*Preaching in an Age
of Globalization*

Preaching in an Age
of Globalization

Eunjoo Mary Kim

WESTMINSTER
JOHN KNOX PRESS
LOUISVILLE · KENTUCKY

First edition
Published by Westminster John Knox Press
Louisville, Kentucky

10 11 12 13 14 15 16 17 18 19—10 9 8 7 6 5 4 3 2 1

Book design by Drew Stevens
Cover design by Eric Walljasper, Minneapolis, MN

Library of Congress Cataloging-in-Publication Data

Kim, Eunjoo Mary.
  Preaching in an age of globalization / Eunjoo Mary Kim.
      p. cm.
  Includes bibliographical references (p.   ) and index.
  ISBN 978-0-664-23369-3 (alk. paper)
  1. Preaching.   2. Globalization—Religious aspects—Christianity.   3. Christianity and culture.   4. Cultural pluralism.   5. Sermons, American—21st century.   I. Title.
  BV4221.K56 2010
  251—dc22

                                                                        2009040206

PRINTED IN THE UNITED STATES OF AMERICA

∞ The paper used in this publication meets the minimum requirements
of the American National Standard for Information Sciences—Permanence
of Paper for Printed Library Materials, ANSI Z39.48-1992.

Westminster John Knox Press advocates the responsible use of our natural resources.
The text paper of this book is made from at least 30% postconsumer waste.

Contents

Foreword

Teachers of preaching have been wrestling with the fragmentation of listener identity due to gender, age, disability, ethnicity, culture, religion, and class for many years now. There are now homiletics texts and essays that treat nearly every aspect of human difference imaginable. In each instance, scholars identify unique exegetical and theological issues for the preacher. What Eunjoo Mary Kim accomplishes in *Preaching in an Age of Globalization* is not to analyze further the impact of diversity on preaching but to begin the process of identifying how we can be in global *solidarity* across differences. Her aim is to unify diverse theologies and hermeneutics in a common concern for humanization.

I have appreciated Eunjoo Mary Kim's writing for several years, especially her book on preaching in the Asian American context and her history of women's preaching. I had not realized how important and far-reaching her ideas were, however, until I was writing my recent book *Preaching Words: 144 Key Terms in Homiletics.* As I revisited her books and scholarly essays, I discovered them to be pivotal as I dealt with such difficult homiletic terms as "hermeneutics," "multiculturalism," "pluralism," and "gender." In each instance, I found her homiletic knowledge to be broad and her conclusions carefully considered, helpful, and filled with insight.

When I began reading *Preaching in an Age of Globalization*, it was soon clear that her range of interests had culminated in a work of timely significance for the discipline of homiletics. It seems appropriate for this book to be published during Barack Obama's presidency, while we recover from a time when issues of identity and difference pose the clear threat of further fragmenting people here and around the world. In this context, how can we support a common theological agenda from the pulpit, one that is endowed with God's grace and promises renewal and hope for all people? This, it seems, is precisely the question *Preaching in an Age of Globalization* answers on behalf of working preachers and students of preaching.

Recently I volunteered to drive a busload of homeless folk from downtown Nashville to our church to spend the night. As we pulled up at the church, the woman seated next to me in the van asked, "What are you doing this for?" Fumbling for an answer, I replied, "Well, I don't know, exactly. But I hope you might do the same for me." She grinned and then nodded her head and said, "I might." It occurs to me that this feeble interactive paraphrase of the Golden Rule and what we "might" do for one another in a diverse local and global context catches something of what *Preaching in an Age of Globalization* is about. The *mutually* humanizing gospel that we "might" live into together is at the center of the gospel that Kim wants us to preach. Kim shows us how to discover a deeply humanizing message in biblical texts and our many diverse contexts, and how to proclaim that message as the key to understanding and bridging local and global contexts. In essence, she puts us face-to-face with one another across all differences and hopes that we will discover the image of God that has been lost, and discover the hope for the full redemption of our humanity that can be found in Christ.

—*John S. McClure*
Charles G. Finney Professor of Homiletics
Chair, Graduate Department of Religion
Vanderbilt Divinity School

Acknowledgments

In completing this book, I have had many people help me along the way. Above all, I wish to thank my husband, Joseph, and our two children, Dorothy and David, who sustained me with their unfailing love, patience, and encouragement. No words can fully express the depth of my admiration, gratitude, and love, especially for Joseph.

This book could not have been completed without the invaluable support of the Iliff School of Theology, where I teach. I am deeply indebted to Iliff for granting me a yearlong sabbatical leave, which was the stimulus for this project. I am also indebted to Ewha Woman's University Graduate School of Theology and Yonsei University Graduate Union of Theology for allowing me to teach preaching courses during the first semester of my sabbatical year and to research the book's theme in a Korean context. Very special thanks to Professors Paul Huh and Eun-Mi Paik, who invited me to teach at their schools. I am also profoundly grateful to my sister-in-law, Kyung-Ja Lee, and her family for hosting my two-year-old son and me at their home while working in Korea. Their kindness and generosity made my stay in Korea unforgettably rewarding.

I would like to acknowledge the indispensable help of my research assistant, Gi-Chul Kim, for his tireless and diligent work. I am also appreciative of the unerring intelligence and enthusiasm of Beverly Leach, whose meticulous proofreading made my writing as clear as possible.

Finally, I wish to thank my editor, Jon Berquist, and other staff at Westminster John Knox Press for helping me bring this project to completion, for their wise and knowledgeable counsel, and for making this project available to the public.

Introduction

Today, a dramatic shift has occurred in both our individual and communal lives, where we find ourselves moving into a new world, characterized by globalization. The term globalization covers a wide variety of elements. It can refer to the global spread of economic markets, to instantaneous communication across the planet, and the relocation and integration of diverse cultures outside their geographical origins. In an age of globalization, people feel that they are living in increasingly complex ways in a web of interconnectedness as part of a global family.

Christian communities are not exempt from the influence of globalization. In their everyday lives and along the path of their faith journey, Christian believers experience interconnectedness with others from all over the globe. Thus, they face a multiplicity of new pastoral and theological challenges posed by globalization, which are unprecedented in Christian history. How can we succeed in living as a global family on a planet where a small minority takes life for granted, while at the same time life is the one thing that the great majority cannot take for granted? How can the planet become a home for all, for nature as well as human beings? Is a different world possible, a world that strives "to make and keep human life human in the world"?[1] These are just a few critical questions Christian preachers must answer. This new phase of human history characterized by globalization challenges preachers to critically evaluate the ethical and theological responsibilities of all believers; to do otherwise risks making globalization a new form of colonialism. And as they plan the content and style of their contemporary Christian preaching, critical and theological insights into the social and cultural contexts that exist in a globalized world are indispensable prerequisites.

Over the last several years, I have turned a good portion of my scholarly attention to globalization and to researching the relationship between the gospel, culture, and proclamation in this changing context for preaching. For me, Christian preaching is a disciplined effort to understand and express our intentions clearly, precisely, and effectively as we speak about God. Preaching is a theological act. Its task is to represent God as a living reality in our present-day globalized world. Since the term "theology" (*theos-logos*) means "'words' or 'speech' about God—'God-talk,'"[2] we should approach preaching as a theological act through this medium of God-talk—"actual human speech about God,"[3] in which God is related to or involved in human experience and the world. Thus, preaching should not be pursued as an abstract, speculative discourse about ultimate being, but rather should exist in the living speech of human life here and now. Thereby, proper preaching requires the preacher to be a practical theologian. As such, preachers must "do theology" not only with the mind but also with the flesh. Their theological reflection should include what is sensed physically as well as intellectually in everyday ordinary lives and be communicated not by pen but by embodiment: by performing the message in public with their whole being.

Further, preaching as doing theology or God-talk must no longer remain an internal dialogue within and among organized Christian communities. A Christian message that is relevant to our globalized world is not simply the imaginative conversation between individual minds restricted to the life of the church or addressing special doctrines or dogmas venerated in the church. Rather, it should be a wide-ranging conversation among many voices, beyond the boundaries of individual believers and denominations, representing significantly diverse viewpoints of urgent and crucial issues emerging from the impact of globalization. Therefore, in an age of globalization, the preacher and her message should represent one partner in the dialogue with diverse people, worldwide, regarding all aspects of their public lives.

Based on this theological proposition of preaching, this volume presents "transcontextual preaching" as a new homiletical paradigm relevant to the changing context for preaching in the era of globalization. Transcontextual preaching is firmly grounded in Reformed theology, in which God's revelation precedes human faith. Transcontextual preaching thus presupposes the revelation of God, a certain faith that God has in fact revealed Godself. It then develops homiletical processes for reflecting on life and interpreting human experiences, as ways to discern the will of God for the world. The trans-contextual approach to preaching is not *a*contextual, but is thoroughly contextual by transcending the local context in an effort to embrace the larger world as the context for preaching. It goes *through* and *beyond* locality to engage in a global world, where local contexts become interwoven.

In the process of developing a set of homiletical theories for transcontextual preaching, a variety of research methods are applied to the interaction of material, problem, context, and practice. Such approaches as empirical and reflective, analytic and correlative, sociological and phenomenological, hermeneutical and analogical, and deductive and inductive are eclectically employed to produce a new paradigm of homiletics.

The book's five chapters present the theories of transcontextual preaching by exploring its five distinctive characteristics. The first chapter explains the necessity for a new contextual approach to preaching in a globalized world by critically reviewing contemporary homiletical approaches proposed in Leonora Tubbs Tisdale's book *Preaching as Local Theology and Folk Art*,[4] and James R. Nieman and Thomas G. Rogers's cowork *Preaching in Every Pew: Cross-Cultural Strategies*.[5] While their contextual approaches are invaluable resources for understanding preaching in association with local congregational culture, I envision transcontextual preaching as a complement to their homiletical theories, appropriate for the globalized context in which we live.

The second chapter first defines the context for preaching as the locus of God's revelation, then critically analyzes the impact of globalization, and finally challenges the preacher to rethink the task of preaching in a worldwide web of interconnectedness. The locus of God's revelation is explained in relation to three areas—the *koinōnia*, the whole world, and the margins of the world. The current impact of globalization is analyzed as the major factor influencing the contemporary context for preaching and is evaluated in four dimensions—neoliberal capitalism, cultural diversity, environmental decline, and the advancement of information technology.

Chapter 3 concentrates on the theological mandate for preaching, with regard to the issues and concerns emerging from the phenomena of globalization. Among numerous theologians who are invited to the conversation in this chapter, the Reformed theologian Paul Lehmann is the primary dialogue partner. His theological perspective of humanization offers insight into developing a theology of humanization as the theological foundation of transcontextual preaching. The theology of humanization—characterized as liberation, a communal process, solidarity, and the politics of God—involves some homiletical implications for transcontextual preaching that are explicated in three aspects: the formation of a shared identity, the nurture of apperception, and strategic planning for preaching.

The fourth chapter provides a point of view for reading the text transcontextually and develops hermeneutical methods to create the fusion of horizons as a way to transcend locality. Transcontextual hermeneutics proposed in this chapter is a way to search for the truth by reading text and context as Others and employing such hermeneutical methods as an interpathic approach, communal reading, and a paradigmatic interpretation. Transcontextual hermeneutics is in essence a political act, sensitive to power dynamics among various readers and requiring of the preacher a theological commitment to community, society, and the world, with political responsibility and ethical accountability.

Sensitive to diversity in the listening process among the listeners, the last chapter deals with rhetorical strategies for transcontextual preaching. It explores how to address a variety of issues emerging from globalization to listeners who are in varying stages of understanding those issues. As a way to negotiate diversity, the rhetoric of appeals is suggested as the most effective communicative method. The rhetoric of appeals is explained in three respects. First, it is not a mode of persuasion, but a mode of appreciation by appealing to or pleasing the listener. Second, the rhetoric of appeals is aesthetic, stimulating an imaginative awareness of awesome wonder and evoking an appreciative response to that. The aesthetic dimension in preaching is explored in the threefold concept of beauty as sublime, God's primary attribute, and human experience. As practical guidelines for transcontextual preaching, strategies for the rhetoric of appeals are suggested, including a concern for angles, a triadic path of appeals, and language. Finally, the chapter concludes by presenting the beautiful image of a kaleidoscope as the best metaphor for transcontextual preaching. Compared with other cultural metaphors for negotiating diversity such as the melting pot, the salad bowl, and the mosaic, the image of a kaleidoscope is the most appropriate metaphor for describing an openness to inclusiveness and the dynamic interaction of different experiences among the listeners. Therefore, transcontextual preaching, like the beauty of a kaleidoscope, is understood as an aesthetic experience, shared with others in the Spirit of God. Transcontextual preaching as kaleidoscopic preaching calls the listeners who are living in an age of globalization to be multifariously beautiful to others, just as God is beautiful for us.

In addition to these chapters, four sample sermons of my own are included. Portions of these sermons are quoted throughout the book to illustrate relevant points. Each sermon is preceded by some introductory remarks and a brief analysis.

Considering how widely globalization is recognized these days as a vivid reality for contemporary Christians, I hope this book contributes to deepening our understanding of contextuality, making it possible to develop the Christian message beyond the limits of locality. Furthermore, I hope that the practical theological guidance for preaching in an age of globalization offered in this book will be a conversation starter about this new phase of homiletics, appealing in a useful way to a wide audience, from preachers and local church pastors to professors of preaching and seminary students.

CHAPTERS

1

Contextual Approaches to Preaching

The theological task of Christian preaching is to proclaim the gospel to the present of every age and thereby represent God as a living reality in the world. The incarnational nature of the gospel has continuously challenged preachers to interpret a biblical text in ways that will have contemporary historical and cultural relevance. To do so within an appropriate context, in a framework that is meaningful to the congregation, is an ongoing challenge to the preachers.

Despite the contextual nature of Christian preaching, traditional approaches to homiletics have not paid sufficient attention to this aspect of preaching.[1] One reason is that Western homiletical theories are rooted in Greco-Roman rhetoric, which focuses on the speaker rather than the listener, relegating the latter to an arbitrary crowd of individuals with no special relationship to the speaker. Since the early centuries, this speaker-oriented approach has directed homiletical theories[2] and instructed Christian preachers to focus on speaking in a logical manner rather than concerning themselves with how listeners hear as a corporate body of believers.[3]

However, since the 1971 publication of Fred Craddock's book *As One without Authority,*[4] contemporary American homiletics or the "New Homiletic"[5] has shifted emphasis from speaker to listener. Contrary to the traditional deductive approach with the "three-point-and-a-poem" style based on Aristotelian rhetoric, Craddock proposes an inductive mode that begins with a particular experience the listeners

3

have had and leads them to arrive at their own conclusions. In inductive preaching, Craddock explains, the listeners' personal and communal experiences are not merely aids to proclaiming the gospel but also the media through which they can reach a general truth. While the goal of deductive preaching is to effectively deliver the preacher's own theological knowledge to the listeners, who passively receive the message unilaterally from pulpit to pew, inductive preaching aims to help listeners change or transform their lives by participating as active agents in the preaching event. To achieve this goal, preachers are challenged to take the congregational context seriously because how the listeners hear is directly related to who the listeners are.[6]

An awareness of the active role of listeners in the preaching event has stimulated contemporary homiletics to pay special attention to the context for preaching. The development of congregational studies through a variety of scientific methods in the field of practical theology has provided contemporary homiletics with significant resources for understanding the congregation in relation to ethnicity, race, gender, class, sexuality, theological orientation, denominational tradition, and so forth.[7] Moreover, feminist theology and liberation theology, which have emerged since the 1970s, and postcolonial approaches to missiology and contextual theologies in current theological discourses have challenged contemporary American homiletics to reconsider the preaching event "contextually."

Among the homiletical resources dealing with the contextuality of preaching, two books stand above the rest. One is Leonora T. Tisdale's *Preaching as Local Theology and Folk Art*, and the other is James R. Nieman and Thomas G. Rogers's *Preaching to Every Pew: Cross-Cultural Strategies*. Both books have contributed greatly to the growing concern for the contextual nature of preaching by applying their different contextual approaches to preaching. The following two sections of this chapter analyze and critically evaluate the theories regarding the nature of contextual preaching and its methodology proposed in these two books. The last section concludes the chapter with a brief remark demanding a new paradigm of contextual preaching as context changes under the forces of globalization.

PREACHING AS LOCAL THEOLOGY AND FOLK ART

In her book, Tisdale focuses on the congregational culture as a major component of preaching. Based on the Roman Catholic theologian

Robert Schreiter's *Constructing Local Theologies*,[8] James Hopewell's *Congregation: Stories and Structures*, and other scholarly works written by contextual theologians and anthropologists, Tisdale proposes that both the nature and method of preaching should be understood from a contextual perspective.

The Nature of Contextual Preaching

Tisdale insists that Christian preaching should in its nature be fundamentally a "highly contextual act of constructing and proclaiming theology within and on behalf of a local community of faith."[9] She calls such an act "contextual preaching."[10] Contextual preaching considers the unique culture (or subculture) of the congregation to be central—not peripheral—to its concern and requires preachers to become "amateur ethnographers" or cultural anthropologists, "skilled in observing and in thickly describing the subcultural signs and symbols of the congregations they serve."[11] Therefore, the task of the preacher is to "exegete" not only the biblical text but also the unique subculture of the congregation.

Contextual preaching aims toward "greater 'fittingness' (in content, form, and style)" for a particular congregation as well as "greater 'faithfulness'" to the Christian gospel.[12] These goals require the preacher to become not only a local theologian but also a "folk artist" who is able to express local theology through "symbols, forms, and movements that are capable of capturing and transforming the imaginations of a particular local community of faith."[13] In this sense, Tisdale defines contextual preaching as local theology and folk art.

Contextual preaching as local theology and folk art is, states Tisdale, "cross-cultural communication"[14] between the preacher and her congregation, for the preacher speaks to the people of a different subculture from that of her own. Like missionaries in foreign lands, the preacher relates to the congregation as both an "insider," who becomes acculturated into the life of a particular local congregation, and an "outsider," who has grown up in a different subculture; thus, the preacher is able to notice the distinctiveness of the insiders' subculture that they may not be able to see.[15] The roles of the preacher as both insider and outsider can be envisioned using three different images: the prophet who judges the existing local theology, the poet who transforms the imaginations of the congregation, and the theologian who evaluates the local theology in a larger church tradition.[16]

The Method of Contextual Preaching

Throughout the book, Tisdale focuses on the cultural identity of a congregation and attempts to understand it through a symbolic approach to cultural analysis. For her, culture is, as anthropologist Clifford Geertz defines it, "an historically transmitted pattern of meanings embodied in symbols . . . by means of which [human beings] communicate, perpetuate, and develop their knowledge about and attitudes toward life."[17] Each congregation has its own distinctive subculture, expressed by an "idiom"[18] or a unique web of signs and symbols, which involve both verbal symbols (stories, jokes, sermons, favorite hymns, oral and written histories, and church publications) and nonverbal symbols (ritual acts, architecture, gestures, and visual acts). The unique subculture of a congregation, according to Tisdale, binds it together and at the same time distinguishes it from other congregations, and this unique subculture is the context for preaching.[19]

To discern the distinctiveness of a congregation's "subcultural identity" with its particular "worldview, values, and ethos,"[20] the preacher needs practical advice to identify and exegete these symbols. Tisdale provides some useful guidelines for dealing with such verbal and nonverbal symbols as stories, interviews, archival materials, demographics, architecture and visual arts, rituals, events and activities, and people.[21] Throughout the rest of the book, she offers insights into how one should interpret congregational worldviews, values, and ethos. She suggests strategies for connecting the world of the biblical text to the congregational context, and shows the preacher how to design sermonic forms as folk art.

Critical Reflections

Tisdale's book is groundbreaking for contemporary homiletics: it is the first homiletical textbook to provide a concrete model for understanding preaching in relation to a congregational culture. Her symbolic approach to cultural analysis helps the preacher perceive the congregation not as an arbitrary crowd of individuals, but as a corporate body of believers who share a common expression of their faith with one another. Her suggestions and guidelines for homiletical strategies are, on the one hand, very helpful resources for both exegeting the elements of a congregational culture and interpreting its "tick descriptions" while preparing a sermon. On the other hand, it is notable that Tisdale's anthropological approach has some limitations when dealing with issues emerging from the challenges of social changes both within and beyond congregations. Following are some challenging areas of Tisdale's contextual preaching that need further discussions:

1. Postmodern challenges to the modern meaning of culture

In her anthropological approach to a congregational culture, Tisdale presupposes that each congregation, as a unique subculture, is an integrated, unified whole comprised of various elements represented by verbal and nonverbal signs and symbols. This presupposition depends heavily upon the modern view of culture as "internally consistent wholes."[22] According to Kathryn Tanner, however, modern anthropological theories of culture have changed drastically in recent years because of the influence of other disciplines such as history, literary theory, sociology, and political science:

> It is less and less plausible to presume that cultures are self-contained and clearly bounded units, internally consistent and unified wholes of beliefs and values simply transmitted to every number of their respective groups as principles of social order. What we might call a postmodern stress on interactive process and negotiation, indeterminacy, fragmentation, conflict, and porosity replaces these aspects of the modern, post-1920s understanding of culture, or, more properly as we will see, forms a new basis for their reinterpretation.[23]

With its presumptions of stasis and consensus, the modern meaning of culture is unable to deal with conflicts and tensions involved in and between cultures. Tanner critically reminds us that behind the modern view of culture, summing it up as a whole is "the exclusive privilege of the anthropologist's superior perspective,"[24] which prevailed in the study of modern anthropology; one of its major goals was to aid the administration of colonized people as manageable wholes.[25]

Critical insights of the postmodern and postcolonial perspectives into the meaning of culture challenge the preacher to reconsider the nature of culture and the method of cultural analysis. In fact, Tisdale admits that various subcultures may coexist within one congregation, and warns that the preacher should listen closely for any dissonance within a congregation.[26] However, Tisdale does not discuss this further. Rather than elaborating on such issues as how diverse subcultures within a congregation can relate to one another as a whole, or how mar-ginalized subcultures should be treated in describing the general culture of the congregation, Tisdale concentrates on understanding the con-gregation as a monolithic and homogenous group. For example, her understanding of cross-cultural communication means a crossing-over between two subcultures—the preacher's and the congregation's—based on her monolithic understanding of the congregational culture. If conflicts and tensions among various subcultures within the congre-gation are not considered in the preaching event, such preaching is not fully contextual.

2. The dimension of semiotic studies

When explaining her symbolic approach to cultural analysis, Tisdale identifies it with the method of semiotics by stating that she uses the term "symbolic" as a synonym for semiotic, which is not a familiar term for many pastors and laity.[27] In fact, contemporary semiotics is not limited to analyzing and interpreting idioms; rather, it is a far broader field of study in communications, involving many different theoretical stances and methodological tools for analyzing a variety of cultural phenomena.[28] In other words, semiotics is an umbrella term embracing the whole field of communication, including "such broad categories as speech and writing or print and broadcasting, or . . . spe-cific technical forms within the mass media (radio, television, newspa-pers, magazines, books, photographs, films, and records) or the media of interpersonal communication (telephone, letter, fax, e-mail, video-conferencing, computer-based chat systems)."[29] In semiotics, interdis-ciplinary studies are crucial for analyzing communication systems and determining hidden meaning(s) behind the external reality of commu-nication. Rather than seeing communication as a straightforward trans-mission of a message from speaker to hearer, semiotics views meaning as a continual process of creation through the interaction of changing sociocultural, psychological, economic, and historical factors of cul-ture within particular cultural contexts.[30] Therefore, semiotic studies involve investigating the construction and maintenance of reality by particular subgroups within one social group.[31]

Semiotic studies can be useful for recognizing the complexity of con-gregational culture, which is not simply an external reality expressed by signs and symbols but also includes the ideological functions of the congregation. In addition to a symbolic approach, other approaches such as socioeconomic, political, and psychological analyses are also helpful for analyzing the power dynamics involved in the formation of the congregational culture.

3. The changing context for preaching

The forces of globalization are rapidly changing today's world, which raises a key question about the context for preaching in relation to Tisdale's emphasis on locality. If contextual preaching focuses on its locality, what does "local" mean in our global world? Tisdale defines the term "local" as a particular congregation with distinctive, unique cultural characteristics that are different from other congregations. Perhaps local churches in small-scale, rural, or other remote areas, which rarely interact with others outside their communities, might preserve their own distinctive subcultures. However, the majority of Christian churches today have become urbanized and globalized; their members live as social beings in a multiracial and multicultural society on a global scale; and their churches coexist with different ethnic, denominational, and religious communities in close proximity. As a result, it is not realistic to assume that the congregational culture is static or limited to its locality.

Tisdale states that contextual preaching as a local theology does not advocate "localism or creeping parochialism" because "preaching can be both local in its address and global in its vision, both fitting for a particular congregation of God's people and faithful to a transformative gospel."[32] Her statement needs to be fully explained in relation to how local theology can be global in its vision.

4. Theological meaning of the context

The context for preaching is not only anthropological but also seriously theological. More precisely, the context for preaching means not merely the concrete human life, expressed by symbols and signs that imply the worldviews, values, and ethos of a congregation, but also a locus where God is present and acts for humanity. If preaching is to be thoroughly contextual, it must deal with the context as the locus where congregations experience the presence and work of God. Such preaching requires theological discernment as well as cultural analysis, for contextual preaching should be a serious theological act aiming to help a congregation discern what God is doing to make and keep human life human in the given congregational context.

Just as the context for God's presence and activity is open and dynamic, so is the context for preaching. Consequently, preaching that concerns itself exclusively with a particular subculture of a congregation without sufficient interaction with the different racial, ethnic, and religious cultures surrounding the congregation or within the congregation has a serious theological problem, for it keeps the congregants from stretching their experience of the presence and work of God, thereby limiting their search for the truth to their particular congregational context. Today's changing world challenges Christian churches and preachers to extend their understanding of context for preaching and to reconsider the nature and methods of contextual preaching to connect the local with the global.

PREACHING AS CROSS-CULTURAL STRATEGIES

Recognizing the reality of multiculturalism within and beyond the church in North American society, Nieman and Rogers conducted a survey to determine how preaching has (or has not) responded to the cultural diversity of congregational cultures. Over a two-year period, they interviewed a diverse group of preachers who regularly address cross-cultural audiences. They asked twelve questions about how their preaching related cross-culturally to their particular congregational contexts.[33] Based on an analysis and interpretation of the data collected from the interviews, Nieman and Rogers, in their coauthored book *Preaching to Every Pew*, present cross-cultural strategies for preaching.

The Nature of Cross-Cultural Preaching

Nieman and Rogers pay special attention to the challenges of a "multicultural America,"[34] an area long ignored in homiletical studies. Nieman and Rogers use historical review to examine multiculturalism within the United States; they assert that American churches are not exempt from multiculturalism. They find that there are "multiple hearers" within the same congregation, who are diverse in ethnicity, class, and religious diversity.[35] According to Nieman and Rogers, this multicultural reality should challenge preachers to critically evaluate whether their preaching effectively relates to the entire congregation, crossing the boundaries of multiple hearers within the congregation.[36]

As constructive guidance for cross-cultural preaching, Nieman and Rogers suggest that the congregation be understood within the image of "neighbor,"[37] which they describe as follows:

> The neighbor is someone we regularly meet, a fellow participant in social encounters. The word thus designates interaction, not just proximity. . . . [But] the neighbor is clearly not a member of our household. . . . The neighbor, though not a part of our homes, is still a part of our lives and therefore deserves special treatment. The treatment is named at the heart of both testaments in scripture: "Love your neighbor as yourself." . . . To love our cross-cultural neighbor in preaching means sharing the treasure of the gospel we hold so dear. To do any less would be, by contrast, downright unneighborly.[38]

The distinctive biblical meaning of neighbor is evident in the parable of the Good Samaritan:

> In the Parable of Good Samaritan, . . . "neighbor" refers to how we act toward fellow human beings, particularly those nearby and in need. . . . The issue for all preachers is, quite simply: have our words shown us to be a neighbor? . . . If Christ proved to be our ultimate neighbor in his self-empting love on the cross, what does that imply for those who dare to gather as the body of Christ?[39]

For Nieman and Rogers, the ultimate goal of cross-cultural preaching is to reach out to our neighbors, to culturally diverse congregants. The preacher's role is to create a point of contact through preaching to our diverse neighbors who are nearby and in need.

The Method of Cross-Cultural Preaching

Nieman and Rogers focus on the significant role that culture plays in preaching. They state that preaching is "an act of communication . . . inextricably embedded in culture."[40] For them, culture is not a naturally given state but a creative "human construct,"[41] which can be described in three ways: a "process" that is "constantly changing and moving"; a "plural" rather than a "single, monaural" construct; and a "paradox" representing not only the shared agreements that people reach but also "the contest in which commonly held items are given quite different meanings."[42]

Based on this dynamic concept of culture, Nieman and Rogers understand that congregational culture is neither static nor monolithic. It is
not a homogenous group rigidly bound to any one cultural situation,
but a united body of many subgroups that are different in race, gender,
ethnicity, class, age, beliefs, and so forth. No single approach to culture
is sufficient when analyzing its wholeness, and this applies to a congregational culture as well. Because no general strategy reaches all listeners
equally, Nieman and Rogers do not try to propose a single method of
cultural analysis. Instead, they suggest that, to examine different facets
of culture, congregational cultures should be analyzed from multiple
"cultural frames" or angles. Based on their analysis and interpretation of
the data collected from their survey, they propose four cultural frames:
ethnicity, class, displacement, and beliefs. For each cultural frame, they
give instructions on how to determine group characteristics and suggest corresponding preaching strategies. Each cultural frame has its own
point of view when examining the congregational culture and thereby
contributes to a more comprehensive picture, by functioning "like different photographs that display a mountain from many angles."[43]

In interpreting the congregational culture by using these four cultural frames, Nieman and Rogers insist that the preacher be open and
honest. While a symbolic approach is useful to sketch the external
characteristics of subgroups, open and honest conversation deepens the
awareness of particular situations among different subgroups. By means
of conversation, preaching can be a "collaborative enterprise,"[44] which
means a "partnership of preaching"[45] between preacher and congregants
from diverse cultural backgrounds. For example, the preacher might
invite the listeners into the partnership process of sermon preparation
by encouraging them to study biblical texts, explore useful images, and
so forth. The preacher can also offer postsermon discussions to answer
questions and share comments. These discussions can not only allow
alternative voices to be heard and valued but also become a space for
exploring the intersection between preaching and daily life.[46]

Nieman and Rogers remind us that this collaborative conversation
can happen only when the preacher changes herself into an effective
cross-cultural communicator. By opening herself to being more flexible
and by expanding her comfort zone to communicate beyond her own
ethnic background, the preacher can effectively communicate with the
capacity to embrace (or acknowledge and accept) the genuine differences between the subgroups of the congregation and herself.

Nieman and Rogers believe that by using a conversational approach
based on a partnership between the preacher and the congregation's

subgroups, the preacher can discover the diverse cultural perspectives of those belonging to different cultural subgroups. The preacher can find common ground among her congregants by sharing the authentic stories that have been a source of suffering and pain throughout the world. At the same time, the preacher can celebrate with the listeners in the belief that God is the source of all life.[47] In this way, cross-cultural preaching is ultimately a celebration of God's presence and work throughout the world.

Critical Reflections

Nieman and Rogers's work offers constructive homiletical guidance in a multicultural America. They help identify a range of challenges and key issues that preachers face in multicultural settings. Nieman and Rogers's discussion on the nature of preaching and methods for cross-cultural preaching also stimulates further discussion of the following issues:

1. The postmodern meaning of culture

While Tisdale sees congregational culture as a unified whole, based on the modern meaning of culture, and is concerned with cultural differences between the preacher and her congregation, Nieman and Rogers are aware of the diversity existing in a single congregation and are concerned with how to reach diverse subgroups of listeners cross-culturally. Their understanding of culture as a process, a plural, and a paradox is consistent with the postmodern meaning of culture that focuses on the "internal diversity of cultures."[48] From the postmodern perspective, culture is neither static nor monolithic but dynamic and interactive. For Nieman and Rogers, the congregational culture is also fragmentary and multiple, even conflicting and disoriented. Therefore, they try to provide homiletical guidance on how to respond faithfully and relevantly to these postmodern realities of a congregational culture.

However, just as the modern meaning of culture has its limitations for understanding a congregational culture, so does the postmodern meaning of culture. Recognizing the confusion and complexities of different cultures challenges the preacher to restlessly struggle to identify the unity and harmony among diverse subgroups within the congregation. Never-ending internal dissent and rapid social changes may overwhelm the preacher and cause her to continually search for a new congregational identity. Likewise, the postmodern view of culture challenges the preacher to develop new ways of understanding the congregational identity, along with new homiletical strategies for diverse congregational subcultures.

2. The identity of the congregation

Regarding the issue of congregational identity, Nieman and Rogers propose the image of neighbor as a guiding metaphor to better understand multicultural congregations. They point out that while neighbors should be treated with love, as both Testaments command, there exists a big difference between neighbor and family. For example, the Good Samaritan did not join the household of the victim; he aided but remained "distinctly Samaritan even in being the quintessential neighbor."[49] This difference raises an ecclesiastical question: Is "neighbor" an appropriate metaphor to describe multicultural congregations? In fact, nowhere in Scripture is the term "neighbor" used to describe the relationship between congregants. Instead, the Pauline Letters and other writings in the New Testament refer to the Christian church in more intimate, strongly bonded, relational terms, such as the household or the body of Christ, regardless of ethnic diversity within a congregation.[50]

It is also worth remembering that in today's society, there are numerous interracial and interethnic married couples and families with varied cultural backgrounds. For them, the identity of household is not grounded in ethnic and racial homogeneity but in a new relationship created by the sacramental and covenantal ritual of marriage. Even when we say that the church is the household of God, this does not suggest a relationship based on racial and cultural boundaries but a relationship bound by the grace of God in Jesus Christ. The changing context for preaching in a multicultural society, therefore, challenges the preacher to reconsider theological images of the church and creatively reimagine the identity of the congregation.

3. Methods of cultural analysis

While Tisdale approaches congregational culture as a unified whole by using symbolic analysis, Nieman and Rogers classify it according to four cultural frames: ethnicity, class, displacement, and beliefs. They use each frame as an angle from which to view a part of the congregational culture and analyze the characteristics of its subgroups. However, as Joseph R. Jeter Jr. and Ronald J. Allen illustrate in their book *One*

Gospel, Many Ears: Preaching for Different Listeners in the Congregation, four frames are insufficient for perceiving the holistic picture of the congregational culture. Instead, their analysis focuses on gender, age, personality type, and patterns of mental operation as well as ethnicity, race, class, and theological orientation.[51]

Numerous cultural elements, which bring fractions and conflicts into congregations, continually challenge the preacher to consider how preaching can repair and rebuild a vision of unity and harmony beyond any differences in the congregational culture. Consequently, it is crucial to take seriously how to deal with diverse cultural elements effectively when developing a sermon.

4. The nature of preaching in the global context

Considering how global our world is becoming, Nieman and Rogers's penultimate remark about "worldly preaching"[52] merits special attention. As they rightly claim, preaching is "a witness to God's mission";[53] in order to become "worldly" by seeking to witness to what God has done and will do, preaching should accept no cultural boundaries. Instead, centering one's preaching in the world is a prerequisite to witnessing God's boundless mercy and love of the whole world.

Though worldly preaching provides some insight into maintaining a global context, Nieman and Rogers do not fully articulate how cross-cultural preaching in American multicultural settings can be centered in the world. In order to provide practical resources for preaching in a wider global context, their idea of worldly preaching needs more theological and homiletical conversation with regard to the following questions: How can the preaching context be understood globally as well as locally? What cultural frames are useful in understanding the congregational context from a global perspective? How can the meaning of faith emerge from a dialogue between the local and the global?

TOWARD A NEW PARADIGM:
TRANSCONTEXTUAL PREACHING

It is notable that one year after Tisdale's book was published, Schreiter's new volume, *The New Catholicity: Theology between the Global and the Local*,[54] was out as a sequel to his earlier work *Constructing Local Theologies*. In his introduction to the new volume, Schreiter explains that ten years after the publication of his earlier work, his perspective on contextual theology was revised due to the changing circumstances caused by globalization. He defines globalization as the "increasingly interconnected character of the politics, economics, and social life of the peoples on this planet."[55] Globalization, he says, is "the extension of the effects of modernity to the entire world" via global capitalism and the communications technologies that create a network for information flow so that "local cultures receive the elements of the hyperculture and reinterpret them in some measure."[56] The compressing effect of globalization, according to Schreiter, makes boundaries between states increasingly insignificant in the flow of information and capital and calls for "dialogue and mutuality" among different local cultures, for there is no longer any locality that is not touched by outside forces.[57]

Schreiter was one of the first theologians to recognize the importance of globalization in relation to the area of Christian theology. Today, his concern for the impact of globalization becomes an even more relevant and complex theological issue interwoven with socioeconomic and political considerations. Homiletics is also challenged to rethink its contextual approach in relation to the phenomena of globalization. Preaching must take a new direction in its theological perspective and homiletical strategies as it encounters the impact of globalization.

The homiletical works produced by Tisdale and Nieman and Rogers are significant resources for developing a new paradigm for preaching in the context of globalization. Their contextual approaches have, on the one hand, greatly contributed to understanding preaching from the perspective of a congregational culture. At the same time, their critical reflections from the previous sections clarify areas that we still need to concentrate on when developing a new paradigm for preaching in today's challenging context of globalization.

As a complement to their contextual approaches, I propose a "trans-contextual" method. We could label Tisdale's contextual approach and Nieman and Rogers's cross-cultural approach as "intracontextual" in the sense that their methods try to interact primarily with the concerns and ideas emerging from a local context (or congregation). But when we take seriously the interwovenness of the context between the local and the global and consider local issues in the wider contexts of a globalized world,[58] we need to employ a "transcontextual" approach. These two methods are not mutually exclusive in the actual practice of preaching. While the intracontextual method focuses on analyzing the particular situation of a local congregation and, as a result, often fails to be attentive to the fact that the local issues are closely related to those emerging from other contexts, the transcontextual method protects preaching from becoming exclusively locked into its own local context. The reality is, however, that preachers rarely use the transcontextual method in preparing their sermons. This transcontextual method—which moves beyond particularity to reach interdependent relationships between one's own and the contexts of others—is now mandated for the preaching ministry in our globalized world.

The next four chapters will present a new paradigm, called "transcontextual preaching." The concept is described in four areas: The context, a theology, hermeneutics, and styles of preaching. Each chapter addresses a related topic with creative theological imagination and innovative homiletical strategies.

2

Globalization and the Context for Preaching

Preaching happens in a context that shapes the lives of both the preacher and the listeners. The term "context" has numerous connotations that affect the understanding of this word. Contemporary social theorists, anthropologists, and ethicists have employed any number of terms for the definitive meaning of context, including community, civilization, culture, society, and social structure or social location. Viewed from the perspective of a particular discipline, the word may be used provisionally and thereby involve a number of limitations. Yet within the range of semantic associations, context plays an important role in framing any theological articulation for preaching.

Which dimensions of context are important for preaching today? This chapter concentrates on the significant influence of globalization, as its dimensions frame a better understanding of the context for preaching. We are now facing dramatic changes throughout the world because of globalization. No longer an option, globalization is an unavoidable reality, no matter where we live. Globalization has made the world an extraordinarily complex yet singular place, drawing us together into a network of relationships, no matter if our congregations are in Denver, Colorado, or in Seoul, Korea. Globalization has significantly impacted local congregations not only in economic and political but also in social and cultural terms. Therefore, an essential and urgent task for preachers is to relate that reality to our Christian faith with the conscious awareness that the context for preaching is the entire world, interconnected economically, culturally, ecologically, and socially. Interpreting context through the lens of globalization requires a trans-contextual approach that moves beyond parochialism and regionalism.

The first section of this chapter explores the theological meaning of context, since it is the locus of God's revelation. Where God is present and works for humanity should be the real context for preaching. The next section explains the phenomenon of globalization and critically evaluates its multidimensional impact on the contemporary context for preaching. And the last section summarizes the theological and homiletical challenges that globalization poses in that web of local-global interconnectedness.

CONTEXT AS THE LOCUS OF GOD'S REVELATION

Understanding context in light of the ministry of preaching is profoundly theological, for the context for preaching is where we experience and witness the presence and acts of God, the source of life. Etymologically, "context" denotes interwovenness or braiding. From the Latin verb *contexere*, meaning to "braid," "weave," or "connect," the noun "context" precludes anything that is divided, stands outside, or confronts. Rather, it suggests a holistic entity in which a vast variety of social and natural factors at the local and global levels are interwoven in a complex manner.[1] A context is neither selective nor fixed, but dynamic and interactive; its constituents are constantly changing.

The context for preaching is inextricably bound to the notion of interwovenness. Preaching is often considered to be an event that happens in a particular social setting. However, this particularity does not mean exclusion. A specific context for preaching is interwoven with a variety of constitutive factors and shares a common denominator with a wider context. On the one hand, the multilayered nature of context often makes it difficult to determine the parameters and characteristics of any given context. On the other hand, the same nature of context makes it inevitable to consider particularity in local contexts. In nearly every aspect of our lives in today's rapidly changing world, local contexts are demonstrably more interdependent with one another than ever before. Yet increasingly, most disciplines in a globalized world require us to take into account the growing nature of interconnectedness. Preachers need to be sensitive to global interwovenness when analyzing their congregational subcultures. At the same time, in preparation for preaching, they should be familiar with a transcontextual approach that integrates particularity with global realities.

The interwoven nature of context is important in the process of discerning the truth in our postmodern world. Though the modern view seeks for the foundations of truth by means of a clear, logical, and univocal way within the limits of reason, the postmodern view criticizes this generalizing approach. It suggests instead that the search for truth should be an ongoing conversation, for our various understandings of truth are parts to be included in a larger whole.[2] God remains a mystery beyond human comprehension, and the truth we perceive is not a comprehensive account but rather a fragmentation of truth, because the locus of God's revelation is beyond our boundaries. The mystery of God encompasses the whole world; it is not limited to our boundaries. As Marjorie Suchocki claims, "The God who is present to us is present to others as well. The God who guides us guides others also; the God who cares for us cares also for others. The whole world is touched by God, and therefore the world can mediate God's presence to us."[3]

Nonetheless, our perception of the truth is limited to our finite experiences and reason. Even our languages are so limited that the expressions we use often distort our understanding of the truth or create misunderstandings. We know the truth selectively from our own viewpoints, within the boundaries of our unique situations, through our distinctive ways of thinking, and in our limited languages. As a result, our interpretation of the truth is always conditioned by our particular situations. When something outside our experience, reason, and language is inaccessible to us, our fragmentary knowledge of the truth cannot proceed toward wholeness unless we deliberately and continuously attempt to broaden our understanding of the truth. One way to stretch beyond our boundaries is to have direct and indirect dialogue with people whose social and personal situations are different from our own. By reflecting on our fragmentary knowledge of the truth as a result of interacting with others in a wider world, we can broaden the horizons of our knowledge and experiences of the truth.

If the ultimate concern of preaching is to help listeners search for the wholeness of truth, and if the context for preaching—the locus of God's revelation—is interwoven into the wider human and natural world, where should the preacher go to discern the revelation of God? At least three domains exist in which the preacher can search for the divine presence: the *koinōnia*, the whole world, and the margins of the world. The *koinōnia* is the starting point.

The *Koinōnia*

Although some preaching events happen outside the church, the majority of preaching is practiced in a particular local congregational context. As Paul Lehmann accurately claims, the true nature of the congregation can be described as the *koinōnia*, "the fellowship-created reality of Christ's presence in the world."[4] In the *koinōnia*, each individual member is invited into the fellowship of maturity in love and in togetherness. The diversity of the members in terms of race, ethnicity, gender, sexuality, age, theological orientation, and so forth expresses the reality of fellowship as a microcosm of the larger world. The *koinōnia* as the community of true disciples of Christ is the context in which the preacher can experience the real presence of Christ, for God reveals the divine will to the members of the *koinōnia* and makes the wisdom of God known to them through their "apperception."[5] Therefore, the point of departure for discerning the revelation of God is the *koinōnia*.

Yet, the *koinōnia* is neither identical to the empirical reality of the visible church nor separable from that church. In other words, not all visible churches in the world are the contexts for discerning what God is doing in and for the world. Instead, as Lehmann asserts, the *koinōnia* is, "the little church within the Church, the leaven in the lump, the remnant in the midst of the covenant people."[6] Only those churches that represent the true church, in which Christ is present, can concretely experience the dynamics of the divine acts for reconciliation and transformation; only in this setting can the members of the *koinōnia* discern the revelation of God in their personal and communal lives.

The Whole World

Although the *koinōnia* is the primary place for the preacher to perceive the revelation of God, God's revelation is not limited to the *koinōnia*. Lehmann reminds us of God's freedom to self-manifest to the whole world:

> There is, of course, one marginal possibility which must always also be kept in mind. . . . The marginal possibility is that God himself [*sic*] is free to transcend—*ubi et quando visum est Deo* ("where and when it pleaseth him [*sic*]")—what he [*sic*] has done and continues to do in and through the church. God's action and God's freedom are never more plainly misunderstood than by those who suppose that God has acted and does act in a certain way and cannot, therefore, always also

act in other ways. Of course, God is bound *to* what he [*sic*] does and
has done. But he [*sic*] is not bound *by* what he [*sic*] has done.[7]

God's action and freedom are so mysterious that they go beyond our
plain understanding or imagination. Whatever God is doing in and
through the *koinōnia*, God is doing also in the world. The God of
the *koinōnia* is also the God of politics and social lives throughout the
whole world.

Therefore, we should not limit the presence and work of God to
Christian fellowship. God's revelation is not restricted to the events in the
Scriptures, traditions, or historical facts of the past, nor is it found exclusively within the Christian community. Rather, God's self-disclosure is
apparent beyond the Christian church. God's liberating activity from
the past extends graciously to our present and even into the future by
the continuing transforming works of the Holy Spirit "to make and to
keep human life human in the world."[8] The creation stories, the history of the people of Israel, and the life, death, and resurrection of Jesus
Christ in the Scriptures are very important, nevertheless, because they are
genuine parables through which we can discern God's continuing activity of grace throughout the whole world, now and in the future. Here,
the whole world means not only human communities but also the world
of nature. Nature has been the medium of God's revelation in various
ways throughout all time and space. In fact, the preacher often finds the
answer to the question "What is God doing in the world to make and
to keep human life human?" outside the Christian community because
the whole world belongs to God. What, then, is the difference between
Christians and non-Christians? Lehmann answers this question by stating that both believers and unbelievers belong to Christ; the difference
between them is not a matter of church membership. The only difference
between them is that for believers, as members of the *koinōnia*, the king-
ship of Christ is revealed, while among unbelievers it remains hidden.[9]

The Margins of the World

A practical question for the transcontextual preacher is, "Where in
the whole world can I experience and discern the presence and work
of the Spirit?" In response to this question, it is crucial to recognize
that God is especially present at the margins of the world, "in the least
expected place, in the midst of sinners in the company of the poor, in

the deep hiddenness of the cross."[10] Biblical stories in both the Old and New Testaments attest that God is present at the margins of society. God stands for the individuals and communities who are set apart from mainstream society on the basis of position, wealth, health, and so forth. A reversal of the social order is anticipated as essential to the coming of God's reign. God's incarnation in Jesus of Nazareth affirms that the margins of society are in fact at the core where the Spirit of God is working on reconciliation and transformation.

Margins are inherently defined by a center and are generally understood to be passively receptive and responsive only to what happens in the center. This negative perception is found in the traditional definition of marginality, which means "alienation, liminality, status inconsistency, powerlessness, or exclusion from the system of labor; . . . self-estrangement, meaninglessness, and normlessness."[11] The determinants of marginality are usually classified as race, ethnicity, gender, class, age, economic status, occupation, education, sexual orientation, religion, and so forth.

However, it is notable that the Asian American theologian Jung Young Lee defines the term "marginality" in a positive sense. According to Lee, marginality is not subjected to or dependent on centrality. Instead, marginality has the potential to create a new reality through dynamic interaction between differing worlds. Jesus' life illustrates this positive side of marginality. Jesus lived in the margins, not as a victim but as a person liberated from marginalization. He saw and thought of himself as someone from outside the mainstream and understood things from the perspective of marginality. For Jesus, the margins were not the borders of centrality but the "creative core,"[12] where he experienced the presence of God and the dynamic life-giving power of the Spirit. Through his life, death, and resurrection, Jesus lived an exemplary life and brought reconciliation to the world between the margins and the center.[13] Jesus' life shows us that margins are the real centers, for where the Spirit of God is present and at work is always at the center. Jesus' life invites us to this creative new center to become God's partners. Even those who belong to the dominant center of a society are free to choose to live in the margins, the new creative core, the locus where God and humanity work together to transform the world.

This awareness that the margins of society are the places of God's revelation challenges us to look deeper into our world today. The radical transformation of the world, in the form of "globalization," has both positive and negative implications for our individual and collective lives. Under these conditions, one of the important tasks for the preacher is to identify the margins of society globally as well as locally and to discern the presence and work of God everywhere to make and keep human lives human.

In the actual practice of preaching, the three domains of context— the *koinōnia*, the whole world, and the margins of the world—are not independent from one another but are interrelated. Often when preparing a sermon, one of these domains can be given priority over another, but eventually all three should be considered as the context where the preacher must search for the wholeness of the truth. The members of the *koinōnia* need to extend their experience and understanding of the truth by hearing the Spirit of God, who is universally present and continues to work for the inclusive well-being of all human communities, especially at the margins of the wider world. For this goal, the preacher also needs to listen to the marginal voices not merely within her own congregation but also among different communities of faith and even among those in the margins who do not participate in a community of faith.

When the preacher broadens the context for preaching from the margins of the local to the margins of the global and follows the lead of the Spirit to discern its diverse activities in the world, her preaching is fundamentally transcontextual. Transcontextual preaching makes it possible for listeners to search for the wholeness of truth by experiencing, feeling, and recognizing how God is present and what God is doing in the world. It often surprises listeners to discover God's grace in different cultural and religious communities in the world.

DIMENSIONS OF GLOBALIZATION

The overarching reality of our time is a global flow, presently referred to as "globalization." We, living in the twenty-first century, are experiencing the interwovenness of the context for preaching in real terms more than ever before because of the rapid pace of globalization. Though it is true that there has never been a time in history unaffected by global impact, today we feel drawn more closely than ever into a global network of relationships, regardless of where we live. Thus, it is impossible to think about the context for preaching without considering globalization.

Globalization is not a univocal concept: its expression reveals the multidimensionality of human existence. The literature about globalization defines it variously by giving priority to one or another domain of human life. For example, while the economic domain has recently become the central issue of globalization, Roland Robertson and others reject the prevalent concept of globalization from that perspective, insisting that globalization be understood in balance by attending to cultural, religious, ecological, technological, and other domains of globalization.[14] More significantly, how to understand globalization is a matter of perspective. From which social position and status and from which theological point of view one stands profoundly determines how one understands globalization.

According to *The Encyclopedia of Globalization,* the term globalization is distinct from similar terms such as "globalism" and "globality." The term "globalism" has been narrowly used to refer to a "political ideology" that supports extending the Anglo-American model of nineteenth-century liberal capitalism to all regions of the world. The underlying norms and values of globalism are based on "a number of core concepts and prescriptions such as individualism, consumerism, market liberalization, deregulation of the economy, and unlimited accumulation of capital," which have been further reinforced by neoliberal capitalism in the late twentieth century.[15] The term "globality," by contrast, refers to "a condition" of a global age, including the widespread interconnectedness of human beings and the global consciousness of the entire planet. The origin of the term "globality" can be traced back to 1512, when the Polish philosopher and scientist Copernicus demonstrated that the earth was not the center of the universe, but that planets existed in a heliocentric, Sun-centered universe.[16]

Compared with globalism and globality, "globalization" is a relatively new word, coming into use during the latter part of the twentieth century. It connotes a "process" or a "trend" of becoming global.[17] Globalization is a "conduit of trade, culture, travel, economics, knowledge, science, and technology" with a "fundamental change in the scale, intensity, and speed of these processes due to enormous advances in the technology of travel and communication."[18] Since the 1990s, "the idea of becoming more global"[19] has become a new ethos that influences people, cultures, and societies. In a single word, the term "globalization" summarizes a wider spectrum of experiences shared by many people from consumerism and market forces to cultural diversity, environmental issues, and technological innovation, particularly in the areas of data processing and communications. Globalization has caused "deterritorialization" by accelerating the worldwide relations that individuals and nations now have beyond their geographical territories.

The realities created by globalization are deeply related to today's context for preaching. It is an essential task and surely an urgent assignment for preachers to examine its impact on their preaching contexts. However, no single approach is sufficient when trying to comprehend the multidimensionality of globalization, for globalization as a cultural determinant in today's world should be seen as a series linking semiotic domains: religious, economic, political, social, sexual, and so on. In addition, the conditions of globalization should be analyzed by means of phenomenological and empirical approaches. In order to present a realistic picture of the interwovenness of the context in today's era of globalization, I will analyze the phenomenon of globalization in four dimensions: neoliberal capitalism, cultural diversity, global climate change, and the advancement of information technology.

Neoliberal Capitalism

Neoliberal capitalism is a revival of eighteenth- and nineteenth-century English liberalism, with both its reduction of humanism and a global extension of its ideology and policies.[20] The idea of neoliberal capitalism is grounded in a "materialistic utilitarian anthropology" that defines "the human being as *homo economicus*,"[21] in which humans are seen as autonomous rational subjects who act solely to maximize their individual self-interest, meaning their economic possessions. The maximization of economic wealth is equated with human well-being and hence with happiness. The supposition is that the more one has, the better off one is. Possessions are also equated with consumption. Consequently, the more one consumes, the better off one is. Based on this hypothesis, market freedom is encouraged as a means of maximizing individual consumption. Any controls placed on the market by governmental regulations or any institutional rules or laws are considered to diminish human happiness and well-being.[22] It is believed that the protection of individual property and the maximization of individual profit can benefit the individual as well as the larger society.[23]

The ideology of liberal capitalism has become the foundation of economic globalization or so-called neoliberal capitalism from the late twentieth into the twenty-first century. Neoliberal capitalism—which aggressively embraces the open market and free trade by enforcing market liberalization, deregulation of the economy, and individualistic consumer-oriented market strategies—has extended the ideology of a global economy and become the force of growth for transnational corporations. International political agents, lawmakers, and the U.S. military support transnational corporations, which in turn fund or support political candidates, parties, and international economic agencies in various ways. For example, the Bretton Woods institutions[24]—such as the International Monetary Fund (IMF), the World Bank (WB), and the World Trade Organization (WTO)—have all functioned to benefit transnational corporations by establishing trade rules regarding tax breaks, corporate subsidies, the removal of trade barriers, and the privatization of such public-sector enterprises as transportation, energy, telephones, and electricity, the removal of minimum wage laws, and so forth.[25] The program of structural adjustment, for example, has forced developing countries to repay their debts at high interest, consequently creating an upward spiraling of the debt trap. Moreover, the WTO has set market rules that prevent trade barriers and enforced new rules that keep local governments from protecting their own financial institutions and property interests against takeovers by foreign corporations. International market rules, such as Trade-Related Investment Measures and Trade-Related Intellectual Property Laws, allow corporations to patent the genetic properties of seeds and plants, thus preventing local farmers from producing their own seeds and plants, which has been central to local agriculture for thousands of years.[26] In addition, the U.S. military has functioned as an arm of U.S. corporations. As a recent example, the U.S. military dismantled the state-controlled economies in Afghanistan and Iraq and allowed American corporations to take them over.[27]

Practitioners of neoliberal capitalism have convinced the world that open and free-market economics will reduce poverty throughout the globe, thereby maximizing the happiness and well-being of individuals by satisfying their economic self-interests. However, the consequences of a global economy based on neoliberal capitalism suggest different realities. First of all, the eighteenth-century liberal notion that humans are autonomous rational egos who seek to maximize their individual economic possessions does not appeal to every human being but rather only to the educated, propertied classes of a society. Nonpropertied people, such as hourly waged workers, peasants, and colonized indigenous peoples, constitute the majority of the human population on the planet and are excluded from this possibility, since they do not own individual economic possessions capable of being maximized. As a result, neoliberal capitalism based on eighteenth-century liberalism does not benefit all human beings.

A second reality is created by neoliberal capitalism: although it assumes that the individual and corporate profits gained through global capitalism will result in bringing benefits to the larger society, these gains are not sufficiently shared. Instead, the hierarchies of wealth are more extreme than ever before as people experience the widening gap between the haves and the have-nots, the globally increasing power of the wealthy few over the majority of others, with no reduction in the number of people living in abject poverty.[28] The gap between rich and poor has steadily grown, with some 85 percent of the wealth of the world in the hands of some 20 percent of the world population, much of that concentrated in the top 1 percent.[29] According to World Bank figures, from 1990 to 2005 the world population has increased 15 percent, to 5 billion people. In 2005, more than 20 percent, or 1.1 billion people, lived in extreme poverty, suffering from hunger, early death, disease, and so forth, subsisting on less than $1 a day.[30] More realistically speaking, says Rosemary Radford Ruether, "while a Nike worker in Asia makes less than $2 a day, Nike CEO Phil Knight owns stock worth $4.5 billion, and Nike's 1999 revenues were $9 billion."[31]

In fact, poverty is not limited only to developing countries. People in industrialized countries also live in abject poverty and are subject to many of the same economic dynamics. Transnational corporations do not share with people in their home countries the profits gained when they transfer production and human services to low-wage countries. This unequal distribution of profits causes many critical issues such as excessive costs for social services, a decline of the middle class, a lack of future for young people, and an increase in the crime rate, especially in depressed areas of many metropolitan regions.[32] Nowadays, over 100 million people in North America, Western Europe, Japan, and Australia are living below the official poverty line.[33]

A third reality that neoliberal capitalism creates is that the governments of developing countries have largely lost their national sovereignty. Many developing countries are deprived of their right or ability to pass laws to protect their own national industries or shape their own development and foreign policies. The devaluation of local currency, the sharp rise in interest rates on loans, and the loss of local industries, agriculture, and public sector enterprise are out of their control.[34] Today, countries that do not possess appreciable raw materials or are unable to offer worthwhile markets are ignored and drop out of the global market. The loss of governmental sovereignty in developing countries worsens their economies and contributes to perpetuating extreme poverty in developing countries.

A fourth reality created by neoliberal capitalism is the commodification of the human relationship to the earth and the ecosystem. Neoliberal capitalism, based on the view that the earth's resources are nothing more than a collection of fungible commodities to be exploited for human use, encourages transnational corporations to search for access to such natural resources as water, food, clean air, genetic resources, and even the DNA codes of people. Transnational corporations have rushed to stake out property claims either by achieving legal ownerships or by obtaining intellectual property rights to "hot" commodities. This ongoing search creates a monopoly of natural resources that are essential for human life without regard for social justice, environmental issues, or public health concerns.[35]

The commodity relationship and the market value system extend to relationships among people. People are often judged only by their market value or by what they can perform or afford. Two of the most popular root metaphors (or symbolic language)[36] in our society are "marketplace" and "progress" (or materialistic success). The former values codes of behavior that presses people to compete in maximizing profit and use of labor, and the latter encourages people to be optimistic about the global economic system.[37] Both metaphors are popular not only in secular society but also in religious communities. The ominous fact is that many churches themselves are governed by these metaphors. An increasing number of Christian churches regard churchgoers as consumers and adopt market values and tactics to their church-growth strategies. Their main concern is to offer the kind of services that will attract more consumers of religion. For example, most megachurches provide their "customers" with space not only for worship and fellowship but also for shopping, dining, sporting, entertainment, and leisure. In relation to worship, many churches try to lure religious consumers by offering a "popular, casual, contemporary, media-inspired worship," paced to "high standards in the secular marketplace."[38] Their sermons stress materialistic, success-oriented individualism based on the pop psychology of positive thinking; their music touches a surface level of worshipers' feelings; and their prayer time utilizes superficial entertainment such as MTV. A commodity culture reinforced by neoliberal capitalism endangers all human relationships not only in churches but also in families, neighborhoods, schools, and other human communities. In addition, orienting human relationships on a market value causes severe personal, communal, and environmental problems by weakening the capacity of human communities to integrate socially.

Neoliberal capitalism is deeply embedded into our daily lives at all levels. Contemporary congregations experience global dehumanizing consequences in their personal and local contexts and need guidance in order to redirect their economic values regarding property, work, consumption, taxes, insurance, and social welfare. Concerning this issue, preachers are challenged to reconsider the global economy from the perspective of the living economy of God (the *oikonomia tou theou*). This perspective encourages both the preacher and the congregation to envision alternatives to neoliberal capitalism and engage in making radical changes.

Cultural Diversity

Cultural globalization has become more prominent since the second half of the twentieth century. Technological advancements in the communication and transportation industries, the continuing urbanization of much of the world's population, and an interdependent global economy have intensified cultural flow. Culture, which "minimally refers to the ways in which people give meaning to their lives,"[39] consists of many types of symbols that human beings learn from social life. Through globalization, the planet becomes "a social location in its own right," rather than territorial spaces.[40] People experience a "smaller" planet when their social lives spatially expand. A vast variety of global culture can be reached locally through the Internet, movies, satellite and cable television shows, CNN, global sports such as the World Cup and the Olympics, and through such international businesses as Coca-Cola, Starbucks, and McDonald's.

In addition, frequent transnational migratory movements reshape local culture. Globally, the number of migrant workers is increasing. More people in developing countries cross borders to find jobs in wealthy countries. Politically and religiously oppressed people and victims of war are increasingly moving to Europe and North America to find refuge and asylum, safe from violence. At the same time, people from wealthy countries are emigrating, following profits from the global economy and market forces. An increasing number of people from developed countries are traveling all around the world for a short- or long-term period. As people experience a new sense of living in a compressed, smaller world, their worldviews, values, and lifestyles change, and eventually their local communities change as well.

A small town, Clarkston, six miles east of Atlanta, Georgia, in the United States, is one example of radical social change caused by globalization. Social and cultural changes in Clarkston began in the late 1980s, when resettlement agencies selected the town as a place for refugees to begin their new lives because of the geographical and economic advantages Clarkston had, due to its proximity to Atlanta. Before the refugees began arriving, Clarkston was a mostly white, "sleepy little town by the railroad tracks."[41] But soon, this town of 7,100 has become one of the most culturally diverse global communities in North America. As many as half of its residents are now refugees from war-torn countries around the world: Afghanistan, Bosnia, Burundi, Congo, Gambia, Iraq, Kosovo, Liberia, Somalia, and Sudan. Clarkston High School now has students from more than 50 different countries; the local mosque draws more than 800 attendees every Friday; and there is a Hindu temple as well as Vietnamese, Sudanese, and Liberian Christian congregations. At the shopping center, Vietnamese, Ethiopian, and Eritrean restaurants and a halal butcher closely line the streets.[42]

The multicultural reality caused by globalization creates a global connectedness or a sense of sharing a single space. On the one hand, the awareness of changing social dynamics caused by cultural diversity can contribute to a change of consciousness, enriching people's views of their community in an embracing way. On the other hand, cultural diversity in a local context can create conflicts and divisions between older and newer residents of a community, and foster feelings of fear or threats between the groups. The resistance to learning new ways of living with cultural diversity is often reinforced by the systemic forces of racism, ethnocentrism, sexism, classism, homophobia, and so forth. Moreover, the repugnance of the Other can be intensified for both those who have power and those who do not, for a peaceful multicultural reality requires the powerful to suspend the privilege, status, and power they have enjoyed, while the powerless must transform their patterns of protection and defensiveness into patterns of mutual engagement.

One of the negative consequences of globalization in Clarkston is that continuing conflict exists between the continuing residents and the resettled refugees. Many longtime residents have left town. Many others who have stayed are resentful, ever mindful of the ways in which they believe their lives have been altered because of the refugees. At a town meeting in 2003, with the stated goal of how to foster understanding between the refugees and ongoing residents, the first question submitted anonymously was "What can we do to keep the refugees from coming to Clarkston?" A few years later during the summer of 2006, the mayor banned playing soccer in the town park, an activity that only the refugees in town enjoyed. For many longtime residents in Clarkston, soccer was a sign of unwanted and threatening change. Thus the mayor, in this transparent decree, prohibited the game.

But there is also a positive consequence of cultural diversity in Clarkston. The International Community School, a new public charter school, was founded in Clarkson in 2002 as "a local, and particular transnational space."[43] The original organizers of this school recognized the struggles of the local county schools to cope with such a large influx of refugee children from many different countries; they observed the problems of language, cultural expectations, behavioral norms, and so forth that were overwhelming the traditional public education system. They saw that "one-way assimilation into a homogeneous American culture" did not work in a globalized local context like Clarkston, so they built a multinational and multicultural learning space for local children as well as refugee children.[44] Both parents and students of ICS experience a global society in this new space, where they share their stories, languages, and religious beliefs and respect the religious and cultural differences among themselves. They negotiate their individual and communal identities, "continually react[ing], adjust[ing], respond[ing], creat[ing], and re-form[ing] their identities and lives."[45] Elizabeth Bounds and Bobbi Patterson regard this school as a model of "global civil society in a microcosm" and view this institution as an ideal global "community in diversity."[46]

The most challenging issue emerging from cultural diversity is identity. During the process of rapid social change that results from globalization, personal and collective identities are neither fixed nor formed in isolation. Despite what anthropologists tell us, they are not simply self-generated, pure, and unadulterated. Instead, identity today involves an unending process of negotiation. For example, within the complexities of their cultures, people struggle to define and understand the concept of home for themselves. They search for more secure cultural footings by interacting with others and self-consciously combining various cultural elements to create new systems of meaning and ways of living.

The traditional "melting pot" metaphor is no longer appropriate for the process of forming identity. First used in cultural theories in the United States over a hundred years ago, during America's period of greatest immigration, the term implies that new immigrant groups must shed their native cultural patterns and commitments and be remade into something new, as dictated by the Anglo-Saxon social visions and value system. However, newly arrived immigrants living in the United States in the current era of globalization do not want—nor are they even able—to abandon their cultural DNA in order to become part of the fabric of American life. Rather, identity is formed by going through the highly complex processes of "hybridization" and "glocalization" (or global localization).[47] Hybridization means combining cultural ideas, concepts, and practices into a new hybrid form. Through this process, cultural identity becomes hybridized through the interplay of cultural heritages among racially and ethnically diverse groups. This process is often creative and spontaneous. Glocalization embraces both the local and the global. A local context is not possible without an awareness of a larger, global context in which our locality is placed, for our homes, communities, and churches are globally sustained. However, local culture does not merely adopt those outside factors. Instead, through a complex reflexive process of resistance, appropriation, subversion, and compromise, a local culture constantly reconfigures its new characteristics to create a new identity.

Cultural diversity greatly influences and challenges the context for preaching. An increasing number of Christian churches are experiencing cultural globalization within their congregations and encountering problems similar to those of the town of Clarkston. Globalization destabilizes individual and congregational identities and creates the need to construct new ones. Some churches are struggling to maintain their racial, cultural, and linguistic homogeneity and trying to stem any cultural flow within their congregations; others are actively responding to the changing context for ministry by embracing the vision of racially and culturally pluralistic communities. They are revising their mission statements and restructuring their ministerial systems to be culturally inclusive.[48]

Unfortunately, few churches are active or proactive in responding to the continuing sociocultural and ethnic changes in North America. According to a recent study, 94 percent of churches in America are homogeneous, sharing one predominant race or ethnicity, and maintaining a separation from other groups.[49] In fact, many church-growth theorists have called ethnic homogeneity a positive element in the growth of churches and advised church planners and church revivalists to use the "homogeneous unit principle" as part of their strategy.[50] When we remember that the 2000 census data suggests that, by the year 2050, the United States will have no single majority race or ethnicity,[51] it is ironic that Christian communities founded in diversity within the body of Christ are among the most segregated groups in society. In the midst of some tendencies to segregate culture within the church, preachers are challenged to be sensitive to their changing context for preaching. They need to examine at what stage of identity formation the congregation finds itself and help them envision a new identity from a theological perspective in which diversity and differences are perceived as respected gifts.

Global Climate Change

Global climate change is one of the negative phenomena of globalization. The current crisis of environmental decline is closely related to neoliberal capitalism, which is the stronghold of economic globalization. The ideology of a dominant market economy regards nature merely as a lifeless commodity, denying its active properties that live holistically with humans, and using these commodities in what leads to short-term profits without regard for self-sustaining ecosystems. Both industrialized and developing countries treat nature with depredation, exploiting its raw materials and suffocating it with their garbage.

Air pollution, one factor of global climate change, has a deadly impact on the world ecosystems as it accelerates the greenhouse effect on the earth. The scientific evidence behind global warming is unequivocal. Yet in its fourth assessment of global warming, released on February 2, 2007, the United Nations Intergovernmental Panel on Climate Change used its strongest language when drawing a link between human activity and recent warming: "Most of the observed increase in globally averaged temperatures since the mid-20th century is *very* likely due to the observed increase in anthropogenic greenhouse gas concentrations."[52]

The greenhouse effect is caused by such molecules as carbon dioxide, methane, chlorofluorocarbons (CFCs), and nitrous oxide, which pick up some of the energy that is being reflected off the earth and reradiate it as heat. Without this greenhouse effect, the planet would never have warmed enough to allow life to form. But as ever-larger amounts of carbon dioxide and other heat-trapping gases are released, corresponding with the development of industrial economies, the earth is blanketed and kept warm at an accelerated rate.[53] If greenhouse gas emissions continue at or above their current rate, many changes in the global climate system would happen during the twenty-first century.

Among greenhouse gases, carbon dioxide is the main one to increase the temperature. Which country has emitted the most carbon dioxide over the past century? The United States. With 4 percent of the world's population, the United States has been the top country emitting carbon dioxide. However, according to the recent data collected in 2007 by the Carbon Dioxide Information Analysis Center for the United Nations, the United States is the second with 20.2 percent of the cumulative carbon dioxide emissions while China is the top with 21.5 percent of the world total.[54] Canada, Australia, Western Europe, Russia, and Japan also have high levels of emissions. Altogether, the industrialized world contributes up to 90 percent of the greenhouse gases while the remaining countries are responsible for varying amounts.[55] It is worth noting the German theologian Jürgen Moltmann's criticism of industrialized countries:

> If everyone were to drive as many cars as the Americans and the Germans, and were to pollute the atmosphere through as many toxic emissions, humanity would already have suffocated. The Western standard of living cannot be universalized. It can only be sustained at the expense of others: at the expense of people in the Third World, at the expense of coming generations, and at the expense of the earth.[56]

Global warming has a variety of fatal effects on human life and nature. From Greenland to the Arctic in the north, in the south to Antarctica, and in the mountains such as the Alps in Europe, the Rockies in Canada and the United States, the Himalayas in Asia, the Southern Andes in South America, and Mount Kilimanjaro in Africa, many ice fields and glaciers are melting so fast that half of the glaciers have vanished in the last twenty years, and the total ice area has shrunk by 30 percent.[57] Melting polar ice caps and warmer waters cause sea levels to rise. By 2100, sea levels are likely to rise between 7 to 23 inches, and the changes now under way will continue for centuries to come.[58] As a result, more natural disasters will occur, such as droughts, violent downpours, flash floods, and so forth, and the fresh water supply will diminish. Moreover, people in many big cities in the world will in increasing degrees continue to suffer from acute respiratory problems and related diseases such as lung cancer. In addition, the heightened pace of climate change threatens wild plants and some animals with extinction.[59]

Though wealthy industrialized nations are the primary polluters, poor nations, who cause relatively few emissions, are the primary victims of global warming. The industrialized countries try to preserve

a clean environment in their own territories by means of technology leg-
islation. They also outsource pollution by relocating polluting industries
to developing countries and selling toxic waste to them. For example,
the Coca-Cola Company has many franchised bottling plants that waste
fresh water and distribute toxic waste containing lead and cadmium.
While some of the plants are in the United States, most of them are
located outside the United States such as China, India, Guatemala, and
Colombia.[60] Nonetheless, the destruction of nature in developing countries has a fatal impact on industrialized countries, for the earth's ecosystems interconnect all parts of the globe. For example, rising sea levels are
not only a problem for small island nations. Sea levels are also expected
to rise along parts of Louisiana and the rest of the Gulf Coast, and ultimately along all coastal areas of the continental United States. A new
federal study of climate change and transportation predicts that during
the next 100 years, the water along the Gulf will rise between 2.5 and
4.0 meters or more, resulting in the permanent flooding of one-quarter
of all major roadways and almost three-fourths of the freight facilities
at ports and airports, including New Orleans International.[61] Therefore, the entire world should heed the alarm sounded by the Alliances of
Small Island States, urging everyone to "watch what happens to us, the
small island states. The threats we face today will not be limited to us
alone. . . . Whatever our fate tomorrow will be your fate the day after."[62]

Another serious cause of global climate change is deforestation.
Deforestation is a growing issue, directly related to economic globalization. Some 58 percent of the tropical forests are located in Latin
America, 23 percent in Southeast Asia and the Pacific, and 19 percent
in Africa. Millions of hectares of these tropical forests are burned or
cut every year for economic purposes. In Latin America, the primary
cause of deforestation is cattle ranching. Central American ranchers
export 85 to 95 percent of their beef, primarily for the fast-food ham-
burger industry in the Untied States. It is notable that in 1976 Volks-
wagen set 25,000 hectares of American forest afire to clear land for
a cattle ranch.[63] Deforestation in Latin America accelerated after the
onset of the debt crisis because Latin American countries promoted
beef exports to repay their debts.[64] In Southeast Asia, countries such
as Thailand, Malaysia, Indonesia, Papua New Guinea, and the Philip-
pines cut their tropical hardwood forests to export to Japan, a country
that alone imports 53 percent of the world's tropical hardwood for use
in construction and paper manufacture.[65] The destruction of the tropical forests results in severe erosion, which in turn triggers flooding, the

extinction of species, a decrease in indigenous Indian populations, and the acceleration of carbon dioxide emissions.[66]

Significant scientific research substantiates the assertion that human manipulation of nature for economic and political reasons is accelerating global climate change. With so many catastrophic consequences for both industrialized and poor, developing countries, the current environmental crisis calls both the preacher and the congregation to have a new relationship with nature, one in which humans and nature are viewed as an interdependent matrix of life. For this task, preachers need theological imagination in order to prevent further abuse of nature and to promote the restoration of more harmonious patterns between nature and humanity by cultivating respect, empathy, and love for nature.

The Advancement of Information Technology

It is not excessive to say that today's globalization began with the advancement of communication and information technologies. Since the 1990s, the rapid development of computer technology has created a "space-time compression." Today, the radical reduction in telephone fees and the extensive use of e-mail have increased worldwide social relations, networks, and systems within which the effective distance is considerably smaller than geographical distance. The speed of communication through satellite transmissions; the explosive increase in computer speed, capacity, and availability to consumers; and the corresponding increase in content of the Internet—all make it possible for the first time to organize a so-called network society that has flexible social relations, independent of territories.[67]

The Internet is now a part of the everyday reality of millions of people around the world. Because of the declining cost of computer technology, the Internet doubles its volume every hundred days.[68] The Internet brings people closer to each other by sharing culture, science, economics, and politics. Through the Internet, we see, hear, and articulate what is really going on in the global human community and the world of nature and even find ourselves intimately bound and motivated by shared commitments. The Internet makes cultural convergence possible by bringing the messages of pop culture and consumer products such as Coca-Cola, McDonald's, MTV, CNN, Microsoft, and so forth to even remote corners of the planet. The Internet also brings the diversity of the world into consciousness by linking traditions, identities, cultures, values, and locales rather than simply homogenizing cultures into one common global culture.[69]

The Internet links people to a wider world with vital information and resources. Although the Internet has unimaginable potential for reshaping our personal and public lives, there are also negative sides to this digital globalization. As Nathan D. Mitchell rightly points out,

> People today are indeed connected but these connections are frequently banal, transient, and fragile, and unstable. A few "clicks" can create a Web page—or destroy it. A teenage hacker with a bit of ingenuity and time on his hands can break into the records of a sophisticated banking system or steal secrets from a nation's classified security system.[70]

Yersu Kim reminds us that the Internet has strengthened the transnational dimensions of crime. International mafias, drug cartels, and terrorist organizations like al-Qaeda have been among the first to take advantage of the advances in communication and information technologies.[71] Computer technology is so deeply enmeshed with global economic forces and political systems that computers and computer skills are now mandatory if one wants to participate in the emerging global economy. Yet the vast majority of people on the planet are excluded from information technology. In this way, the Internet contributes to the widening gap between the rich and the poor. It is estimated that out of a world population of six billion people, only one billion have access to the Internet.[72] Poor individuals and nation-states excluded from a global connectivity or from access to the Internet, on which human existence increasingly depends, cannot survive in the global economy and, consequently, become even poorer.

One of the most challenging issues relating to technological globalization is the radical change in the concept of human community. A network society extends the dimension of human community beyond a geographical territory. In a network society, human community is no longer limited to face-to-face contact. We look at others through digitized pictures and build communities through face-to-screen interaction.[73] New communities mediated by digital technology are composed of people sharing a common interest rather than a common space. In these "virtual communities,"[74] people contact each other electronically while physically living in their own respective neighborhoods or village. In virtual communities, people experience "virtual reality"[75] by interacting with others in realistic ways, albeit via technology.

The Internet also transforms social dynamics. The equal opportunity for Internet users to participate in electronic communication can disrupt or disturb the power structures in and between organizations. Online communication reduces the power of the traditional authorities to control human dialogue while reinforcing horizontal relationships among the users. More often than not, the Internet strengthens the processes of political decision making and contributes to changing public opinions regarding election campaigns and the work of NGOs.[76]

The changing concept of human community and the transformation of social relationships raise a concern among many preachers about what human community is to be and what their local congregations will be like under the influence of technology. To what extent and how will the Internet impact local life? How will local life be integrated into different cultural traditions, given the presence of the Internet? It is worth noting Mitchell's prediction:

> "instead of belonging to a local parish," Catholics of the future might find their congregation in a "worldwide online prayer community" that will result in "a new understanding of community" and will shake the organization of the church profoundly.[77]

No matter if his prediction comes true or not in the near future, many preachers have already been challenged to reconsider the context for preaching in a rapidly growing cyberspace culture. Historically, preaching was transformed by the transitions from an oral to a manuscript culture and from a manuscript culture to the age of print. Preaching today finds itself at a radical transition from print to Web culture. Many preachers already consider their audience to be a worldwide online network society beyond their local congregations. They post sermon manuscripts or audiovisual records of their preaching on their personal and church Web sites, so that the members of virtual communities may access them.

The flip side of a Web-based culture is that it encourages an individualistic approach to religious life and that sermons and other religious information on the Web cannot be controlled. Congregants may pick and choose what they wish to believe and what teachings they wish to follow, without discussing what they learned on the Web with their pastors and other church members. In this fashion, the Web-based culture may prevent believers from seeing their interconnectedness and interdependence with other members of the church; it consequently brings a subtle but profound paradigm shift in the nature of religious communities in industrialized nations.

In our pervasively pro-technology culture, the Internet is often problematic because it is a largely solitary, private, and impersonal enterprise. It is necessary to have an open and critical forum through multifaceted conversations in order to cross-examine the unbounded and uncontrolled technology of the Internet. As they reflect critically on technology, the preacher and the congregation need to analyze and evaluate the extent to which they want to use technology in corporate worship and prayer.

THE CONTEXT: A WEB OF INTERCONNECTEDNESS

The phenomena of globalization bring local congregations into a worldwide web of interconnectedness. Neoliberal capitalism, cultural diversity, global climate change, and the advancement of information technology have made the world an extraordinarily complex and yet singular place, with a set of potentially disturbing "flows" and "reflexivity."[78] Despite the homogenizing trends of globalization, many systems and practices are local, and many local situations remain robust in their resistance. There is no longer, however, any "local" that has remained untouched by powerful outside forces. The local is linked through multiple ganglia of connections to the global and vice versa, each altered by the wider connection. In this fashion, local congregations are not isolated from the global community. They experience locally a variety of sociopolitical, economic, cultural, and ecological issues, each affected by globalization.

The web of interconnectedness between the local and the global challenges preachers to consider the context for preaching from the perspective of "glocalization": What if the majority of their congregants are upper-middle-class European Americans, such beneficiaries of neoliberal capitalism as stockholders, employees, and CEOs of transnational corporations? What if their congregants resist multiculturalism and insist on ethnic homogeneity in their congregational culture? What if their congregants are physically and geographically victims of air pollution and global warming? What if some of the youth of their congregations are highly obsessed with virtual reality rather than pursuing communal relationships with others in the community? The questions emerging from the glocalized context can go on and on.

The preaching context, closely interwoven by glocalized situations, creates numerous issues and concerns and demands on which preachers critically reflect with prudent and ingenious theological imagination. The discernment of God's presence and work for humanity and nature in this context are possible when both the preacher and the congregation struggle together with the question "What does it mean to make and keep human life human in a globalized world?" This profoundly theological question involves such pastoral concerns and issues as these: How do globalizing forces shape the daily lives of the local congregation? How does God want people to live together in church, community, society, and the world at large, especially when world events also play out locally? What kind of alternatives to the existing ideologies of globalization can be imagined? How can preaching help a congregation envision new relationships among people and between the human community and the world of nature?

The task of the preacher is to interpret, shape, and help congregations carry out their vocations and ministries in a globalized world in fresh and deeper ways. When the preacher reflects on personal and social experiences of her congregation through the lens of globalization and explores biblical narratives from the perspective of a globalized world, new meanings and images can be found in the Scriptures that have not caught our attention before. For preaching to be a faithful and credible voice that helps the congregation envision a new world order and hope for the present and the future, we need to develop a relevant Christian theology that embraces critically and constructively both the local and the global. The next chapter concentrates on this theological mandate for preaching, with regard to the issues and concerns emerging from the phenomena of globalization.

3

Humanization and Transcontextual Preaching

The contemporary context for preaching is undergoing tremendous transformations, tensions, and turmoil due to the effects of globalization. Globalization is a complex phenomenon in which consciously or unconsciously we live interconnected and interrelated lives globally. The process of economic, sociocultural, and ecological globalization accelerated by the advancement of information technology blurs geographical boundaries and confuses our sense of culture, identity, and other particularities. While neoliberal capitalism may have enriched some individuals throughout the world, the global economy has actually increased the overall disparity between rich and poor, with dehumanizing consequences. Within globalized culture many individuals and communities suffer an identity crisis where separate human cultures are being rapidly transformed into a single interwoven fabric of human civilization. At the same time, an impending ecological crisis threatens the future of humanity throughout the planet. In addition, the virtual world created by information technology reduces face-to-face relationships and community life, relegating many of us to an isolated, solitary private life.

Dehumanizing events and circumstances around the globe lead us to ask, "Is a different world possible, a world in which justice and peace are truly global?" This urgent theological question challenges both preacher and congregation to reconsider the ministry of preaching from a new theological perspective, enabling us to envision a new world order and engage in making radical changes in the world.

At this juncture, it is crucial to create a new theological paradigm for preaching. The construction of a theology of preaching in a globalized context should begin with some critical reflection on the global human situations that were analyzed in the previous chapter. From there, we proceed dialectically by bringing these realities into a critical engagement with the Christian gospel, always attempting to seek the signs of God's presence and action in our world.

A theology of preaching in a globalized world must be a public theology and not exclusively a church theology because its audience is transcontextual. Rather than remaining an internal dialogue within a congregation or among Christian churches, the theology of preaching must engage with all aspects of public life beyond its local horizon. I call this kind of preaching transcontextual preaching. Transcontextual preaching brings its unique theological perspective to bear on the many and various issues emerging from globalization. By discerning God's presence and gracious work within and beyond the particular congregation, transcontextual preaching mediates the Christian message more faithfully to the present context, thus helping the listeners broaden and deepen their understanding of the truth.

Developing the theology of transcontextual preaching is the subject of this chapter and is discussed in two parts. The first proposes a theology of humanization as the theological foundation for transcontextual preaching. Based on the theological meaning of humanization, the second part develops homiletical insights into the ministry of preaching toward humanization.

A THEOLOGY OF HUMANIZATION

In his book *Ethics in a Christian Context*, Christian ethicist Paul Lehmann explores fundamental ethical issues in relation to what God is doing in the world to make and to keep human life human, and he suggests what we, as believers in Jesus Christ and as members of his church, are to do.[1] The construction of a new homiletical paradigm in our globalized world is directly related to Lehmann's ethical concerns, and its starting point is the search for a theological definition of humanization. What does it mean to make and to keep human life human?" In other words, what does humanization mean in the context of globalization?" A theological understanding of humanization has four aspects: humanization as liberation, as a communal process, as solidarity, and as the politics of God.

Humanization as Liberation

While humanization is not a term exclusive to Christians, Christian Scripture offers a rich source for reflection on the meaning of humanization. From the biblical point of view, humanization means "the liberation of human beings from the present evil age" (Gal. 1:4), freedom from any kind of slavery or structure that diminishes human dignity or worth, including racism, classism, sexism, ethnocentrism, despotism, even our own devaluation or self-limitation. Humanization realizes one's right to be human. Human beings are liberated when they discern the evil of the age in which they live, criticize it, and distance themselves from it.

The Synoptic Gospels describe the life and ministry of Jesus of Nazareth as the model for liberation. The self-giving of Jesus Christ makes freedom possible through the logic of grace by nullifying the logic of the evil age—the Roman law which condemned the innocent man. In him, liberation implies a dialectic between love and freedom. Jesus was free to move from the logic of the evil age and live with compassion for the oppressed on the margins of society. This is exactly the nature of God that Christian Scripture bears witness to. According to the biblical narratives, God's freedom is God's love; God limits Godself through faithfulness to God's promise to love. The christological event reveals God's love for humanity in "the maximum solidarity of God, who takes on history in all its human dimensions: 'born of a woman and under the law,'"[2] and invites us to the struggle for freedom and a new ordering of the world.

Gordon Kaufman, who supports the position of humanist theism, identifies Christian liberation (or salvation) with humanization in the sense that Christian liberation shows us "the direction in which communities and individuals must move if our world is ever to become more truly humane."[3] Based on this Christian concept of salvation, Kaufman defines humanization as "a new creation" or "a new life":

> Notions of reconciliation, love and peace, of self-giving, voluntary poverty, concern for our enemies, vicarious suffering, point to our deep interconnectedness with each other. . . . Paul sometimes speaks of this new Christian orientation in life as being a "new creation" by God, a creation in and through which God is reconciling us to Godself, and calling us to become "ambassadors for Christ" (2 Cor. 5:17–20a). Elsewhere he speaks of a new "Spirit" that enlivens the Christian community, a Spirit the "fruit" of which is "love, joy,

peace, patience, kindness, goodness, faithfulness, gentleness, self-control" (Gal. 5:16, 20–23 [RSV]). The Johannine writings go even further than Paul in their interpretation of the significance of the new life aspired to and experienced within the Christian communities, identifying it as the very presence of God: "Beloved, let us love one another; . . . love is from God; everyone who loves is born of God and knows God. . . . for *God is love*" (1 John 4:7–8; emphasis is mine). The salvation—the relation to God—promised in these (and other) well-known texts is nothing else than the special quality [that] human life is expected to take on within this new community, with its straining toward truly humane patterns of existence within itself, and its larger task of fostering further humanization in the world roundabout through its ministries of healing and reconciliation.[4]

While humanization tends to be understood as the human liberation in political, social, and cultural contexts, we should remember that human liberation is not achieved without human beings living in a peaceful and constructive relationship with their physical environment. Liberation from social, political, and economic injustice must accompany "ecological sensibility that cares for the earth that cares for us."[5] Political and economic liberation and ecological, holistic sensibility are inseparable; they must be interconnected to bring about the fulfillment of humanization. Liberation as a concept that extends to ecological sensibility means healing. Healing is what the great diversity of creatures and life forms needs to survive against exploitation and destruction. It includes healing from the sickness of pollution and of diseases arising from a lack of clean water, from the torture of animals through experiments and in factory farms, and so forth.

Extending liberation to nonhuman creatures receives its theological validation from the metaphor of God's body. According to Sallie McFague, the "resurrection of the body" metaphorically means God's body, the world:

> The world as God's body . . . may be seen as a way to remythologize the inclusive, suffering love of the cross of Jesus of Nazareth. The incarnate God is the God at risk: we have been given central responsibility to care for God's body, our world. . . . To sin is . . . to refuse to take responsibility for nurturing, loving, and befriending the body and all its parts. Sin is the refusal to realize one's radical interdependence with all that lives; it is the desire to set oneself apart from all others as not needing them or being needed by them. Sin is the refusal to be the eyes, the consciousness, of the cosmos. . . .

> In the metaphor of the world as the body of God, the resurrection becomes a worldly, present, inclusive reality, for this body is offered to all: "This is my body."[6]

McFague claims that God's bodily presence in and among us at all times and in all places implies that God is present as the universe. The image of the universe as God's body reconfigures "the self-expression of God," in which vulnerability, shared responsibility, and risk are inevitable. God cares about the world as we care about our bodies, and God relates sympathetically to God's body, just as we relate sympathetically to our bodies.[7]

In our time of globalization, McFague's theological imagination, seeing the universe as God's body, challenges us to rethink the inclusiveness of the gospel. It creates room to embrace the universe, as well as all people, in God's inclusive household. Therein the Christian interpretation of salvation extends to the redemption of nature. As Paul the apostle says in Romans, "We know that the whole creation has been groaning in labor pains until now, . . . while we wait for . . . the redemption of our bodies" (Rom. 8:22–25), and we wait for this hope with patience. In consequence, humanization as Christian liberation has "a tri-dimensional relationship of communion 'with God, with other humans, and with the rest of creation.'"[8]

Humanization as the fulfillment of the liberation of all creatures on earth is a hope in God's coming reign of freedom, justice, and peace for the whole creation. Just as Christian hope is eschatological, centered on anticipation of the reign of God inaugurated in the life, death, and resurrection of Jesus Christ, so is humanization. It is provisional and anticipatory actualization here and now in the new life by the power of the Holy Spirit, until the Christ comes again.

Humanization as a Communal Process

From the perspective of Christian theology, "the social doctrine of the Trinity" provides a theological foundation for understanding the concept of humanization. The social doctrine of the Trinity is based on the concept of *perichōrēsis* (mutual coinherence) of the Trinity. God as the creator, sustainer, and perfecter of our humanity exists as the unity of the Trinity. God is a community of three distinct persons in which they are present with one another, for one another, and in one another, giving themselves each to the other to the world.[9] Miroslav Volf explains the relational entity of the Trinity as follows:

> The one divine person is not that person only but includes the other divine persons in itself; it is what it is only through the indwelling of the other. The Son is the Son because the Father and the Spirit indwell him; without this interiority of the Father and the Spirit, there would be no Son. Every divine person is the other persons, but each is the other persons in their own particular way.[10]

The unity of the community of the Father, Son, and Holy Spirit becomes "a prototype of the human community."[11] When the social doctrine of the Trinity is analogically applied to the identity of human beings, who are created in the image and likeness of the communitarian triune God, their identity is conditioned by their social relations with others. Humans are created to live not as solitary individuals but as relational and communal beings in the presence of the divine Trinity. We cannot live authentically without welcoming the others who vary in race, gender, ethnicity, culture, nationality, and sexuality, for we are created to reflect the personality of the triune God.[12] Therefore, being truly human implies not merely an individual with moral perfection or a private spiritual disciplinary life. Rather, humanization is a communal effort toward the transformation of the human community to become a new society like the perfect community of the Trinity.

It is notable that Kaufman considers the relational and communal nature of human beings as the universal ground in our pluralistic global world. He eloquently articulates his anthropological notion of universality at a "biohistorical" level:

> The word "biohistorical" holds together in one both the biological grounding of our human existence and the historico-cultural dimensions of human life, thus highlighting what is most distinctive in our humanness. . . . Brain-scientist Terrence Deacon argues that the emergence of symbolic behaviors—such as language, a central feature in the historical unfolding of human cultural life—helped bring about the evolution of our unusually large brains. . . . Thus, all the way down to the deepest roots of our distinctly human existence we are not simply biological beings, animals; we are biohistorical beings. And in significant respects, our growing historicalness—our historicity—is the most distinctive mark of our humanness. . . . Our historicity cannot function optimally unless it is working harmoniously with its biological base—our bodies and the ecological net-

works that sustain and support them—and only if that biological base is itself functioning well. Taking responsibility for ourselves and our societies as biohistorical beings must always include, therefore, taking significant responsibility for the organic and physical networks of which we are part.[13]

Like Kaufman, David Kelsey also understands the biological and sociocultural nature of human beings as the universal ground. In his essay "Wisdom, Anthropology, and Humanity,"[14] Kelsey asks, "What is a human being?" and provides a clue to the answer from the canonical Wisdom literature's creation story. According to Kelsey, in canonical Wisdom literature, God creates a society of diverse physical beings, including human beings, not as normatively perfect beings who are free of struggle, damage, pain, and death but with their finitude and limitedness. All creatures are inherently mortal; their resources of physically based energy and of capacities to regulate that energy are temporary. Because of their finitude and limitedness, all creatures must depend on one another for their well-being, even though their interdependence often causes conflict, collision, and damage among them. Therefore, the canonical Wisdom literature understands that God is related to the existence of human society of physical beings and that, of all the creatures, human beings are capable of responding to God's calling to be wise in exercising their finite energies for the well-being of society. Human beings become genuinely free through their calling by God for a life with and for others.[15]

Kelsey finds that this canonical anthropology is consistent with the modern secular interpretation of humanity. Research conducted in the areas of evolutionary biology, genetics, neurology, endocrinology, paleoanthropology, cultural anthropology, and sociology reveals that humans are finite and limited social beings in need of communal relationships. For example, the social sciences view human beings as

> adaptable, anxious, and curious; led by powerful psychological drives and needs for communal identity; liable to violence, mental disease, and fantasy; and embodying ultimate and preliminary commitments to linguistic habits, symbolic systems, and social organization.[16]

Consequently, all human existence—that of every individual woman and man, every community and society—is constituted fundamentally of an interlocking biology, history, and sociocultural situation, whose web of interdependency is integral to its creatureliness. This scientific view of humanity parallels the theological concept of human beings based on the social doctrine of the Trinity and the canonical Wisdom literature. Because humans are created to be communal beings, humanization implies a relational, communal process for the fulfillment of what human beings are intended to be.

In the context of globalization, we increasingly live in a single global village, closely and complexly interdependent and interconnected with all other living beings. At the same time, our global village is faced with racial and religious hostility and the possibilities of ecological and nuclear calamities that could destroy us all. Humanization is a communal effort to construct a new worldwide community to which we all belong and must contribute, so that the community of our global village may be renewed to become the place where every living creature created in God's image dwells as a fellow citizen in the household of God (Eph. 2:12–20).

Humanization as Solidarity

To achieve full humanization as a relational and communal process demands a concrete practice of living together with others. In our globalized world, we encounter a multifaceted pluralism and must come to terms with otherness and difference. The Others—persons of another culture, another ethnicity, another religion, another sexuality, another socioeconomic status, and so on—are among us. They are a "part of us, yet they remain others, often pushed to the margins."[17] We see them daily on the streets as well as on the screen in our living rooms. Some are our colleagues, friends, neighbors, and family members, even our spouses and adopted children. How should we, then, relate to these Others and properly negotiate otherness in order to live an enriched life together?

An abundant life with others is possible only by standing in solidarity with all people. Solidarity is based on the conviction that "each person has become a particular reflection of the totality of others." In solidarity, "each does not simply affirm the otherness as otherness but seeks to be enriched by it" through the praxis of mutual participation and sharing.[18] With solidarity, we suffer with others and seek their fulfillment as part of our own fulfillment. Therefore, as Jon Sobrino reminds us, the word "solidarity" denotes "mutual support among unequals, with all giving and receiving the best they have at all levels: economic, cultural, intellectual, religious. . . . Once this happens, . . . the world [becomes] 'a *home* for all.'"[19] In this sense, solidarity is more than hospitality. Although hospitality is a priceless virtue in any society, it does not adequately constitute full humanization, for hospitality is a temporary relationship between host/hostess and stranger/guest. Separate identities are perceived; boundaries are not crossed, nor is status adjusted. With hospitality, a guest does not expect to belong to the hosting family's household, nor to be considered a member of the family. By contrast, solidarity involves mutual transformation toward a new reality of the global family, wherein we embrace one another as members of the same household, with an expectation of living together forever.

Therefore, this act of mutual embrace makes solidarity authentically different from hospitality. Volf helps us understand the concept of embrace with the analogy of the gesture of hugging:

> An embrace always involves a double movement of aperture and closure. I open my arms to create space in myself for the other. The open arms are a sign both of discontent at being myself only and of desire to include the other. They are an invitation to the other to come in and feel at home with me, to belong to me. In an embrace I also close my arms around the other—not tightly, so as to crush her and assimilate her forcefully into myself—for that would not be an embrace but a concealed power-act of exclusion—but gently, so as to tell her that I do not want to be without her in her otherness. . . . I want her to maintain her identity and, as such, to become part of me so that she can enrich me with what she has and I do not. . . . An embrace . . . mediates and affirms the interiority of the other in me, my complex identity that includes the other, a unity with the other that is both maternal (substantial) and paternal (symbolic)—and still something other than either.[20]

A genuine embrace is possible only through respect and an acknowledgment of another's dignity and worth. More than merely assigning a label to another, explains Thomas Reynolds, respect requires a "response-ableness" to the other's value and demonstrates "genuine commerce with the other" in the form of a responsibility for the meaningful vitality of the other.[21] Through respect, mutual recognition happens, and "justice-making love"[22] for those who are marginalized and excluded emerges as a way to embrace them. In the community of embrace, others are part of our own true and full identity.

The practice of embrace with respect rests on the triune God's openness to and loving inclusion of radical otherness—sinners and the lost.

The entire ministry of Jesus, especially his table fellowship with social outcasts, demonstrates God's embrace of others with respect. While such an embrace leads to solidarity, a refusal to embrace others results in dehumanizing conditions. As Volf adamantly asserts, a refusal to realize one's radical interdependence with others is sin; the real sinner is the one who casts the other out through acts of ostracism, oppression, deportation, or liquidation.[23]

The dimension of embrace is not limited to the otherness of human beings; it includes nonhuman creatures too. Because the Spirit, the source of both biological and spiritual life, embraces "the soil and the stars, the animals and the plants along with all God's human creatures,"[24] we are called to embrace all creatures. Such efforts were already manifested in the incarnation of God in Jesus Christ. God's passion for entering into our world, which is totally different from the Divine, is the model of embrace and solidarity.

Humanization as the Politics of God

Because the dynamics of humanization involves a radical transformation of the community of all creatures, it is reasonable to say that humanization is "making and doing politics."[25] Based on the Aristotelian concept of politics as "the science of the highest or supreme Good,"[26] Lehmann defines politics as an "activity and reflection upon activity, which aims at and analyzes what it takes to make and keep human life human in the world."[27] According to Lehmann, humanization is, on the one hand, fundamental to revolution in the political sense of being "the passion, process, and promise through which happenings in history make room for what is human in people and in society and for what it takes to make and to keep human life human."[28] On the other hand, humanization is definitely different from revolution. While the former is grounded in God's political activity, the latter is a human activity, involving "the risk of violent overthrow" with an accompanying confusion between "promise and disillusionment, celebration and suffering, joy and pain, forgiveness and guilt, renewal and failure."[29] In the process of humanization, God involves Godself as a politician through the events of Jesus of Nazareth, in giving emissaries grace to proclaim

> the unsearchable riches of Christ, . . . the plan of the mystery hidden for ages in God who created all things; that through the church the

manifold wisdom of God might now be made known to the prin-
cipalities and powers in the heavenly places, . . . until we all attain
. . . to mature manhood [sic], to the measure of the stature of the
fullness of Christ.[30]

If God is conducting humanizing events in the world today through
the continuing presence and power of the risen Christ in and over
human affairs, how and where can we find this activity? In relation
to the question of "how?" it is crucial to interpret the story of Jesus
of Nazareth paradigmatically. As McFague explains, the christological
event is "a partial, limited account of the contours of the salvific power
of God in a particular time" and "a classic instance, embodying critical
dimensions of the relationship between God and the world."[31] Thus
the story of Jesus of Nazareth is "illuminative and illustrative of [the]
basic characteristics of [a] Christian understanding of the God-world
relationship."[32] The relevant question for contemporary preachers as
they approach the story of Jesus of Nazareth as the paradigm of humanization is this: In what ways is that story significant for transforming
our globalized world into a truly inclusive world where all creatures
find themselves at home together? In this manner of inquiry, the story
of Jesus of Nazareth provides us with clues for discerning God's continuing activities to make and keep human life human in today's world.

In relation to the question of "where?" it is important to stress that
humanization is not simply a "church" theology; it is open to other
faith communities, including movements for justice and peace in secular society. Remembering that humanization is an eschatological hope
in the coming reign of God, those non-Christian and secular movements can be anticipatory signs and parables of the reign of God. After
all, the consummation of the reign of God means a fullness of life realized by the various and manifest gifts of the Spirit. The presence and
activity of the Spirit are not constrained by the Christian church, but
are discernable in other religious communities and secular society. In
fact, missio Dei means "inviting all religious and non-religious persons
to life,"[33] including those who have a strong commitment to justice
and peace and resist the forces of violence and death in the world.

This pluralistic view of the locus of humanization does not, however, diminish the significant role of the Christian church. When true
to its calling to be the koinōnia, the church is, on one respect, a concrete witness to and an anticipatory presence of God's coming reign.
Through the proclamation of the gospel, fellowship in faith, solidarity

and loving service of those in need, and the planting of seeds of hope in God's coming reign, the church has paradigmatic significance as a fragment of God's anticipatory reign.[34] Christian churches must remember that they are not closed circles of faith but are open to the wider world, where the ongoing activity of the Spirit of life is often found. The church can discern God's politics on a broad scale by seriously engaging in conversation with other religious and nonreligious communities. Therefore, what makes the church be the *koinōnia* in a globalized world is an openness and a long view beyond its own horizon.

PREACHING TOWARD HUMANIZATION

Transcontextual preaching is based on the theology of humanization. Its focus and substance concern the liberation of all creatures from the present evil age and the restoration of a community in which all human beings live in solidarity as the image of the triune God. Therefore, the ultimate goal of transcontextual preaching is to participate in the politics of God by guiding the congregation toward humanization. Toward this purpose, two urgent tasks emerge: the formation of a shared identity and the nurture of apperception. How, then, can our sermons fulfill these tasks? With regard to this question, the theology of humanization encourages the preacher to make a strategic plan to become engaged in transcontextual preaching.

Preaching as the Formation of a Shared Identity

Forming a shared congregational identity, as one task of transcontextual preaching, begins by recognizing that congregational culture and tradition are not an internally coherent whole but share multiple heritages and allegiances. Many preachers and congregations tend to assume that a congregation has a collective identity based on such commonalities as race, ethnicity, and sociocultural backgrounds.[35] Yet the reality is not as it may seem. Congregational identity is actually "a series of hyphenations," infused with "a vibrant and vital element of heterogeneity," and formed through various processes of "adapting to, borrowing from extraneous elements, informed continually by the precarious crisscrossing of cultural boundaries."[36] Thus, congregational identity is an "identity-in-difference," containing an "irrepressible indeterminacy."[37]

In many cases the reality of a congregational identity with this indeterminacy may make the church fragile and unstable, even causing it to
be fractured or divided. Church history shows—and we experience in
our church lives today—that socioeconomic, political, and cultural differences among congregants can cause disagreements over beliefs and
values, and readily engender conflicts and power struggles. How, then,
is it possible for the congregation to be members of the same church?
It is through a shared identity, "a togetherness of differences,"[38] that
urges us, preachers and congregations alike, to create "a public and
mutual space of sharing."[39]

A shared identity is not based on similarity or common ground
regarding race, ethnicity, national identity, belief, or theological orientation. But it is grounded in connections and relationships with others.
In other words, a shared identity is a commitment to sharing otherness
and differences of the people, especially, of the marginalized individuals and communities, without denying existential similarity among different people. This commitment is based on the theological conviction
that all human beings are created to live as a community of different
people in solidarity with one another. In a shared identity, others are
part of our own true and full humanity.

A shared identity is not naturally generated. Rather, it demands of
both preacher and congregation an intentional and deliberate effort
for its formation. It requires a process of building solidarity among
different people and the various activities of their communal dwelling. Just as the essence of communal dwelling is beyond locality in our
globalized world, the essence of sharing must go beyond the boundary
of a particular local church. Because a local congregation is part of the
global body of Christ, it needs to share itself and its differences with
others in the wider world. Thus, a shared identity requires openness to
the genuine experience and value of others in a global context, while
still being primarily faithful to its own local context and discovering
differences among its congregants.

The congregation with a shared identity is distinguished from other
social groups or communities by its underlying commitment to one
shared vision of humanization, into which multiple congregational
voices are connected and bound together. The theology of humanization reminds us that all human beings are created to live as a community in solidarity with others, toward a vision for a new world. Thus, the
congregation with a shared identity is a community of different people
with a common commitment to this vision for humanization, grounded

in hope for the coming reign of God. A shared identity is possible only when this commitment exists strongly within the congregation.

The most effective instrument for forming a shared identity is dialogue, for a shared identity is created when differences are mutually understood with respect. A constructive dialogue can make possible a recognition of differences, a reciprocity of understanding, and eventual reconciliation among different people. Transcontextual preaching aiming at the formation of a shared identity regards the preacher as a dialogue partner with the congregation. The preacher's role is to engage the congregation in an ongoing conversation concerning humanization until it figures out how to live a life together that is dedicated to right action both within and outside of the church.

It is helpful to note Foucault's contrast between polemics and dialogue. According to him, a person engaged in genuine dialogue acknowledges the interlocutor's right to speak, while a polemist refuses to yield that right. In this way, polemics has a "stable and repressive monological character," while dialogue presupposes "the ethical conditions of openness toward the other, . . . of holding open the ideal possibility of agreement and consensus," simultaneously assuming the possibility of disagreement.[40] Reynolds sums up this nature of dialogue as follows:

> Dialogue itself is the art of speaking, of conducting a conversation, of thinking, of question and answer. . . . In the tensional reciprocity of dialogue with an other (the new, the strange, and the known unknown) we learn to recognize and revise our biases and prejudices. This needs not entail agreement or consensus, but it does signify a transpositioning into a common linguistic space, or shared subject matter, even as the other remains other, something at a distance.[41]

The goal of dialogue is to create mutual understanding. Here understanding means the appreciation of something new, something outside our world, something more than what we already are.[42] Yet not all dialogues ensure mutual understanding. The constructive dialogue involves the following six qualities, as Reynolds suggests:

> a willingness (1) to *listen* attentively to what another has to say; (2) to *discover value* in another's way of naming and relating to the mystery of the whole; (3) to *appreciate* and so uphold its value, not remaining indifferent, but imaginatively and metaphorically entering into its uniqueness as it might be seen by the other; (4) to be *challenged* by the encounter facing up to the limitations of one's own perspective in

light of the other; and finally (5) to be *changed* by it, to let one's perspective be supplemented and enriched as a consequence of stepping into the border zone of engagement. Yet in all these forms of "willingness," embrace, precisely as an offering of oneself, means (6) not to efface or deny but to *give witness* to one's own particular standpoint.[43]

In the process of constructive dialogue, mutual understanding happens through argument, confrontation, endurance, appreciation, challenge, and change on both sides. By embracing, sharing, and exchanging differences between one another with respect, dialogue partners expand the horizons of who they are. The formation of a shared identity is possible only through this kind of dialogue.

Transcontextual preaching based on constructive dialogue is a communal activity that presupposes a willingness to risk being with the difference of another. By creating space for the other in the act of preaching, we can look forward to new possibilities of convergence, vital mutuality, and solidarity. Consequently, this preaching has the power to transform the congregation into the *koinōnia*, a fragmentary foretaste of a new reality of humanization.

Preaching as Nurturing Apperception

One of the most important components of the theology of humanization is the discernment of humanizing activities within and beyond the church. Transcontextual preaching is concerned with this theological task and takes upon itself the task of nurturing the listeners' apperception. *The American Heritage Dictionary* defines apperception as "conscious perception with full awareness" or "the process of understanding by which newly observed qualities of an object are related to past experience."[44] In line with this, Lehmann speaks of "apperception" as the capacity of perceiving true humanity and uses this term as a "uniquely human capacity of knowing."[45] Contrary to strictly intellectual learning, apperception occurs within a matrix of an entire human sensibility that includes feeling, willing, and thinking, "without knowing how one has come to know it."[46] Theologically speaking,

> apperception is the experience of self-evident self-discovery through which one is drawn into the heritage and the reality of what it takes to be and to stay human in the world. Apperception is the experience of retrospective and prospective immediacy—whatever may

be its biological and psychological vectors—which shapes and is shaped by the dynamics of human responsiveness to God, world, and society.[47]

Out of apperception, the faculty of judgment arises: we discern "what is humanly true or false" through apperception. So, says Lehmann, "the fulcrum of what it takes to be and to stay human in the world of time and space and things is the nurture of apperception."[48]

When the preacher wants to nurture her listeners' apperception through her preaching, it is important for her to know that the nurture of apperception does not happen randomly but through critical theological reflection and effective communications. Critical theological reflection entails a threefold dialectical process. First, the preacher critically sees the listeners' existential situation in the sociocultural and politico-economic context of a globalized world, and identifies the false images of humanity and the dynamics of dehumanizing forces in the world. Second, the preacher probes the theological meaning of humanization against dehumanization, and then presents true images of humanity, with new insights into humanization created from the perspective of the theology of humanization. And finally, the preacher interprets a variety of humanizing activities within and beyond Scripture and the Christian Church to be the parables and fragments of humanization, to which the listeners are invited to experience a foretaste of a new reality of humanization.

In the first step of the dialectical process, God's activity in the Bible, especially in the events of Jesus Christ, functions as the measuring stick for a critical analysis of globalization. The story of Jesus of Nazareth is the parable or the paradigm of what God is doing in the world to make room for the freedom for and fulfillment of humanization and provides a lens for us to see the world aright. The current trends of globalization critically evaluated through this lens reveal some false images of what is human. First of all, the figure of "*homo consumptor*," with the catchwords "I consume, therefore I am,"[49] distorts what it means to be human. *Homo consumptor* is a product of consumerism, a cultural construct created artificially by the profit-oriented, capitalistic global economy. Defining human beings as intrinsically created with the desire to consume is propaganda with which businesses maximize their profits by pushing people to a constant level of consumption.[50] Moreover, the "technological imperative"[51] inherent in our developed world misleads us by implying that human beings can make everything possible through technology. Without carefully considering whether human technologies might harm human beings and their environment, this technological imperative, based on human arrogance, can endanger the whole world by means of nuclear weapons, ecological destruction, and so forth.

These two false images of humanity collaborate with the assumption that competition underlies all human relationships. Unrestrained competition, however, denies mutuality, precludes solidarity, and eventually destroys the communal nature of human existence grounded in the belief that human beings are created in the image and likeness of the triune God. As José Ignacio González Faus reminds us, in nature "big fishes eat little fishes," but in the human community "'big' people exist to help and raise up, not to eat 'little' people."[52] Insofar as competition is allowed to operate without limits, it undermines the common good and leads to a disregard for the communal welfare. For example, many transnational enterprises outsource their services and products from developing countries to places where they can employ child workers and where social or ecological considerations are nonexistent, in order to line the pockets of a few rich people in the developed world.[53]

In the second step of the dialogical process of theological reflection, the theology of humanization contributes to proposing alternative images of what is human, and to creating humanizing forces based on a true image of humanity. For example, the image *homo consumptor*, prevalent in our culture, leads us to understand human freedom as "the ability to choose among commodity and service options" and to hold property in private and exclusive ownership. Such an individualistic concept of property risks excluding others from access to life and ignoring the humanity of others. However, in the image of humanity created from the social doctrine of the Trinity, humans are relational and communal beings, genuinely free through their calling by God for a life with and for others. This communal image of humanity does not justify property as absolute, exclusive ownership; rather, it helps us understand property in light of "God's economy of graceful giving."[54] For the triune God, who is the self-giver, giving us all things with Godself (Rom. 8:32), property exists for the sake of "reciprocity, redistribution, and gifting."[55] Therefore, human property is "a means of realizing our vocation as a human being," and ownership is "a means of fulfilling our calling to be God's stewards through community with God, other human beings, and nature."[56]

The last step of the dialogical process of theological reflection is to find parables for the true image of what it is to be human locally and globally in our world, as well as in Scripture, and interpret them to be humanizing forces for contemporary listeners. Parables of humanization can be found not only in biblical stories but also in contemporary events and human efforts to transform the current dehumanizing forces of globalization into forces of true globalization, by which justice and peace become truly global. Such activities include price supports to prevent the flight of capital from developing countries, consumer boycotts of exploitative business monopolies, and backing for the worldwide antiglobalization network stretching from Seattle to Cancún,[57] to name just a few.

In order to nurture the listeners' apperception through her preaching, the preacher needs to develop effective methods for communicating her theological reflection with her congregation. Here it is worth noting what Richard Lischer points out: "The key to forming people for discipleship lies not with the hortatory but with the indicative mood of address."[58] Rather than using the imperative mood to say, "This is what you had better do, or else!" the indicative mood persuasively and therefore more powerfully renews congregational life as a way of being and living in truth and solidarity with others. Moreover, rather than prescriptive statements of duties toward humanization, descriptive statements effectively address both what it means to be human in a world that God has created for all creatures, and what happens in the world to fulfill God's promise for a new heaven and a new earth.

Different from forensic oratory, deliberative exhortation, or deterrence, indicative and descriptive language allows the preacher to use such pictorial and imaginative devices as irony, simile, and metaphor, which can stir and inspire the listeners and eventually renew their apperception. The tone of both indicative and descriptive statements is inviting: "Seeing that you are who you are, where you are, and as you are, this is the way ahead, the way of being and living in the truth, the way of freedom!"[59] Such a tone appeals to the listeners' conscience and calls them to voluntarily respond to the sermon by reorienting their worldviews and life values.

Therefore, preaching based on the descriptive and indicative mood gives words of invitation. It describes what God is doing in the world, and in doing so, it creates room for the freedom to trust, commit, and take responsibility for being and staying human in the world. Those who receive the invitation are willing to participate in God's humanizing activity by living out their lives as a new parable of humanization.

Preaching as Strategic Planning

Transcontextual preaching, aiming at the formation of a shared identity and the nurture of apperception, is in essence visionary. It is ultimately concerned with how preaching can transform the world with a provisional yet productive vision of dwelling together in the world. However, such a vision is not achieved by one or two random sermons. Instead, visionary preaching demands strategic planning. An intentionally planned, creative, and imaginative sermon, integrated into other areas of church ministry, can evoke a communal consciousness to humanization and provide concrete ideas and guidance for the actualization of humanization.

In fact, the congregants who listen to a transcontextual sermon want the preacher to be part of their community, to lead, work with, and help them to realize the vision introduced in the sermon. Remembering my preaching experience, this is true. Once I preached the sermon "Surprise, Surprise, Within and Beyond the Church"[60] to the congregation where my family and I attend regularly. The sermon focused on creating a visionary community based on the gospel of diversity in Jesus Christ. After worship, many members came up to me to say, "Thank you for challenging us. Please help us grow with that message." "I am very grateful to you for putting that vision into words. I have thought about that for a long time. I hope you work with us to transform the direction of our church toward that vision." Such responses reveal that transcontextual preaching toward humanization requires strategic planning under pastoral leadership. The congregants who listen to the sermon want the preacher to continue to guide them with follow-up ministerial works. Although a guest preacher can inspire and challenge the listeners to think about a new humanizing direction for their personal and communal lives, the preacher who is their pastor can help her listeners make God's future come true in and through their lives with a deliberate strategic plan.

Coming from the Greek term *stratēgos*, strategy means "the charting of a course of action." It "plots the direction in which an organization should move to position itself to carry out its mission most effectively."[61] In this sense, strategic planning is "a continuous process of designing the most effective means to accomplish its mission."[62] William Hull calls preaching conducted by strategic planning "strategic preaching." According to him, strategic preaching is a call to be pulled forward by God's unfinished agenda in this world. It invites us to live out of that vision Jesus called the kingdom of God, indeed to claim the life of the "new age" here and now "on earth as it is in heaven" (Mt. 6:10). In pointing the way to God's tomorrow, the preacher not only gets out in front of the congregation as a leader but thereby opens up a path that invites the congregation to undertake the journey with its pastor.[63]

Thus, strategic preaching aims to enrich congregational life by providing clarity and urgency to the most basic questions of the congregation's existence and its future: "Why are we here?" "Where do we go from here?" "How are we going to get there?"[64]

Strategic planning creates synergy between preaching and other ministerial programs and integrates them into a unified expression of pastoral leadership. The desired result of each sermon prepared from a strategic plan is to participate in movement toward the ultimate destination of the entire pastoral ministry—the actualization of humanization in the world—with momentum that stimulates and energizes the congregation along the journey together. To reach the ultimate goal, strategic preaching needs to be transcontextual, balancing a strong commitment to building the *koinōnia* inside the local church with an equally strong commitment to transform the wider world that the church exists to serve.

To maintain this balance, the preacher needs to reflect on how the sermon can contribute both locally and globally to the actualization of humanization. To put it concretely, the strategic preacher is, on the one hand, primarily "a community builder," one who works "to mold a somewhat amorphous collection of individuals into a cohesive group"[65] by planting a shared identity among them. On the other hand, the preacher is "an eschatological agent" who anticipates the transformation of the whole world toward humanization and who calls the congregation to join her visionary ministry with passion by living out of the journey together with her.[66] Therefore, strategically prepared sermons should function as "a pathfinder"[67] with which the community can plan a route together to get from where they are to where they need to be as members of the global village. To provide an adequate pathfinder, the preacher needs to use the foregoing dialectical process of theological reflection.

The social doctrine of the Trinity suggests that the preacher's leadership be team based. God functions as a team in the Trinitarian scheme and thereby calls us to do the same. Like the communal character of the Trinity, team-based leadership involves a relationship between reciprocity and interdependence. As Hull clearly explains, it is "a social role that enables a diverse group to act together with unity of will and purpose."[68] When applying team-based leadership to the ministry of preaching, preacher and congregants are partners. Both parties understand the differences between them and share responsibility for initiating and implementing a process. The common interest between the preacher and the congregation does not depend on race, ethnicity, nationality, gender, sexuality, or socioeconomic status but on their shared identity based on their commitment to a new reality of humanization. For this vision to be clearly seen and widely shared, the leadership team must motivate the congregation to take concerted action to actualize its vision locally and globally.

Team-based leadership suggests that preaching be a team ministry. Sermons can be prepared and delivered by a team composed of both the preacher as the pastor and her lay leaders. For example, the pastor organizes a preaching committee as a sermon-formation-and-feedback group[69] with lay leaders and staff members of the church. The input from the group provides significant elements for the preacher to incorporate into her sermons as part of the strategic planning for her entire ministry. The group not only prepares a sermon together with the pastor through Bible and liturgical studies, but also participates in its delivery when the sermon is designed as a dialogue or other conversational form. Two sermons attached to this volume illustrate team preaching. "Remembering the Gift of God (Ephesians 2:11–22)" is designed as a dialogue to be delivered by two people. "Dear Mary and Elizabeth" needs a laywoman who is willing to participate in preaching by singing the Magnificat in the middle of the sermon.

Strategic preaching as a team ministry requires "strategic thinking"[70] on the part of the leadership team in order to guide the church toward implementing God's vision for humanization. Strategic thinking is a process of creative learning by listening intently to the wider world and asking questions that expose a new reality through imagination. Strategic thinking is thus an act of discernment, sensing what is happening throughout the congregation and in the wider world, and seeing how it can participate with God in the world to make and keep human life human. As strategic thinkers sensitive to paradigm shifts in the existing culture, preachers hold both long-range perspectives and short-range viewpoints in their strategic planning for preaching. Through this dual approach, the preacher tries to conceptualize and construct a whole new order of existence: humanization.

CONCLUSION

Transcontextual preaching, which requires serious theological reflection on the full scope of humanization, is all about witness and discipleship across the entirety of life, in and out of the church. It is about reading the signs of the times. We are living in a world filled with dehumanizing factors on both personal and social levels. In the midst of these dehumanizing conditions, transcontextual preaching patiently searches for God's humanizing activities in the world and seeks to understand and embrace the Other, even when that Other exists beyond our horizons.

Therefore, transcontextual preaching is not simply about our commitment to Christ, but also about what that commitment implies for the rest of our lives and for the communities to which we belong. It is an invitation to the listeners to become agents for change, actively participating in the shaping of a new reality of humanization, with the confident assurance that acting on the gospel can make a significant difference in our globalized world. The preacher of transcontextual preaching is called to this vocation, a vocation that strategically "tells the world something about its vocation, even when the world has forgotten or does not want to hear."[71]

4

Transcontextual Hermeneutics

How we understand the truth and discern the will of God poses one of the most challenging homiletical issues of our time. In an age of globalization, this effort is a matter of hermeneutics. Globalization affects how a truthful message for the congregation is discerned and how it will continue to be understood by them. As discussed in previous chapters, human beings in all their diversity are created to live as a community, in solidarity with one another and with a shared vision for a new world. Thus, the truth-claim in an age of globalization should contribute to forging a shared vision and commitment among members of the congregation that are rooted in the theology of humanization.

Biblical hermeneutics and the theological task of humanization are inseparable; often the preacher is challenged to see how her biblical interpretation can create a conversation among multiple congregational voices that will ultimately foster a shared identity among them and establish a foundation for envisioning a new world. Joining biblical hermeneutics with the theological task of humanization allows biblical interpretation to be the principle or bridge by which Christian texts of the past are interpreted and reach an accord with the globalized present. Hence, biblical hermeneutics for the age of globalization is a hermeneutic of humanization.

In this chapter, I propose transcontextual hermeneutics as a hermeneutic of humanization. This does not imply a set of interpretive, theoretical principles for reading a biblical text for an individual reader's private spiritual growth, but rather suggests a guided reading of the Bible in a communal setting for preaching in a globalized world. In other words, transcontextual hermeneutics is a theological conversation that occurs between the biblical text and various globalized human situations, in order to have a "God-talk" in public. The main concern of transcontextual hermeneutics is how to speak meaningfully about God's presence and how to see the significance of God's actions in our globalized world.

Globalization has shifted the locus of theology. We ask, Where is God? What is God doing? To answer these questions, we need to look at the underside of history and the emancipatory struggles of dehumanized people everywhere. Or we need to look at the ecological quest for life's wholeness and integrity. Or we need to look at the world in search of a vision of a new world through a lens of solidarity with others. Transcontextual hermeneutics, then, demands that the preacher read and interpret the text with others from various social points of reference. It aims to read the world "in front of the text," by reading the text not only "within" and "across" local congregations but also "beyond" them in a larger globalized context. In the process of transcontextual hermeneutics, both text and context are equally important and exist in a balanced, reciprocal relationship, and the preacher needs to understand both of them in a new way by means of disciplined hermeneutical skills.

This chapter explores the characteristics of transcontextual hermeneutics in three ways. First, transcontextual hermeneutics understands both text and context as Others. Second, transcontextual hermeneutics uses distinctive methods of reading Others. And last, the nature of transcontextual hermeneutics is political.

TEXT AND CONTEXT AS OTHERS

The Text as the Other

The Bible has been the major source for Christian preaching as the canon of the community of faith. The Bible as the canon is full of images, symbols, phrases, and stories that can play a lead role in shaping and transforming the imaginations of communities into a vision for humanization. As the Reformed theologian Paul Lehmann rightly states, the Bible is "a well of living water" and "an inexhaustible reservoir of the formative images in terms of which the humanization of life may be both conceptually and behaviorally exhibited."[1]

However, to contemporary readers the Bible is also the Other. In the Bible, we read of people whose world is vastly different from our own. We see the authors of the Bible as strangers who inhabit a world of experience distinct from ours in language, culture, worldview, and symbolic referents. Moreover, the knowledge of God revealed in the Bible, especially the actuality of revelation in Jesus Christ, is different from what humans customarily think of and goes beyond the limit and possibility of our way of thinking. Furthermore, rather than dealing with the issues we face in the contemporary world, the biblical text is concerned with God's revelation in its particular historical and cultural context.

The otherness of the Bible leads us to understand that its status as the canon does not have to do with absolutizing the literal corpus of Scripture and its tradition. It is neither "an authoritative depository of revealed truth"[2] nor a timeless, absolute norm for human life. The Bible as the canon of the community of faith is authoritative in the sense that it is to be used as the point of departure for reflection in the faith and life of the contemporary Christian church without ignoring its otherness.

Reading the Bible as the Other is like "a dialogue with a stranger."[3] Just as it is not easy to have conversation with a stranger, so it is with the text as the Other. Strangers who do not share our culture, language, social class, or vested interests put the world together in a quite different way from us. But when we are able to enter the stranger's realm by seeing with the stranger's eyes, we start to understand better what the stranger says to us.[4] Likewise, reading the text as the Other demands perseverance and discipline for us to reach a new worldview where we discover who we are and what we share.

However, for most Christian preachers familiar with a number of basic biblical stories, the Bible appears to be an old friend, a companion rather than a stranger. Yet if we fail to encounter the biblical text as a stranger, our reading risks using the Bible as an instrument for the confirmation of our own prejudices and the status quo. As liberational, feminist, womanist, postcolonial, diasporic readings unfold, the Bible is often misused or manipulated by the powerful, in many cases as a means of oppressing the powerless, the weak, and the marginalized as a result of ignoring its otherness.[5] In particular, preachers in Western Europe and North America—the so-called industrialized countries or the former colonizing nations—must take seriously the Bible as the

Other in order to fully liberate it from sociocultural and politico-economic imperialism.

The Context as the Other

Transcontextual hermeneutics reads the context, as well as the text, as the Other. As presented in chapter 2, the context for preaching in an age of globalization is complex. Economic globalization, cultural diversity, worldwide ecological crisis, along with advances in information technology and transportation, have led the preacher to consider the context for preaching that does not stop at her local congregation but goes beyond it to the global world. Transcontextual hermeneutics does not limit its context to a local congregation but also embraces different groups in a globalized world, for all live in the web of interconnectedness.

Many preachers these days find that posting their sermons on Web sites give more people access to their preaching. In today's world, the effect of preaching extends beyond geographical boundaries, touching otherness and difference in race, ethnicity, gender, socioeconomic status, sexuality, and so forth within and beyond a local congregation. In this framework, transcontextual hermeneutics must consider seriously how different groups read the text and why.

The preacher who reads the text both within and beyond her local congregation is challenged to read it "by way of thinking through others."[6] This is possible only when the preacher engages some aspect of otherness among them. The significance of embracing the otherness of the context in the process of biblical interpretation is based on the conviction that the will of God can be discerned by a variety of different people because the other person is "a 'trace' of the absolute Other, i.e., God."[7]

METHODS OF READING OTHERS

In the process of transcontextual hermeneutics, reading both text and context as Others is fundamental. To prevent them from resigning themselves to the preacher's world, she must respect them for who they are, Others, socially and culturally conditioned Others. However, the ultimate goal for transcontextual hermeneutics is to create new meaning through the mutual transformation toward a new reality of.

humanization for the global family. In fulfilling this goal, transcontextual hermeneutics goes not only *through* otherness and difference but also *beyond* them.

Reading through and beyond others is like an experience of entering into a liminal space. According to the anthropologist Victor Turner, "liminality" is a period of transition.[8] The liminal period is "a realm of pure possibility where novel configurations of ideas and relations may arise."[9] When one enters into the liminal period, one becomes a "transitional being" or a "liminal persona" who is "being initiated into very different states of life."[10] Based on this understanding of liminality, Sang Hyun Lee defines a liminal space as "an in-between space, a 'social limbo' created by a person's leaving his or her social structure and not yet having returned to that structure; or to a new one."[11] Jesus of Nazareth exemplifies a person who entered into a liminal space:

> Working out of his liminal space, Jesus was radically open to his Father's will and lovingly embraced especially the despised and sick people in their mutual liminality, thereby forming a new community, the household of God, as the alternative to the existing social order. Utilizing his liminal freedom, Jesus expressed his infinite compassion to those persons whom society had rejected, crossing again and again the boundaries that the political and religious centers in Jerusalem had imposed on the people. . . . There on the cross, Jesus hung in the deepest abyss of liminality, in a God-forsaken in-betweenness, between his heavenly Father, whom Jesus believed was abandoning him, and the fallen world that betrayed and rejected him. But in this liminality, the costly suffering and thus life-giving nature of God's infinite compassion becomes historically explicit.[12]

For Lee, a liminal space is not merely "a time of ambivalence, ambiguity, and even disorientation"[13] but a creative time, which "enables us to look back into our society and become aware of what is wrong in the way it is organized at the present time."[14] For preachers, a liminal space is a creative time of experiencing new things in worldviews, life values, and other differences. In the liminal space, dynamic interaction happens among the world of the text, the world of the context, and the world of the preacher's own toward a new reality. By dynamic interaction, I mean a dialectical back-and-forth movement or a conversational "fusion of horizons"[15] toward a new understanding of the text. It is a process of meaning-making by thinking through and beyond otherness and difference between the world of the text and the contemporary world. Dynamic interaction does not follow a linear order as the next step after reading the text and the context as Others. Rather, it occurs throughout the entire process of interpretation in the preacher's consciousness until a new crystallization or synthesis of theological understanding emerges from her constructive imagination.

How, then, can the preacher enter into a liminal space? How can dynamic interaction happen effectively and constructively through the entire process of interpretation? In other words, how can the otherness of the text be respected and embraced in an interpretive process in solidarity with others, and in this way participate in creating a new meaning in a liminal space? To read through and beyond otherness and difference requires that the preacher use at least three hermeneutical methods: an interpathic approach, a communitarian reading, and a paradigmatic interpretation. These methods will help preachers to open themselves to enter into a liminal space and have dynamic interaction between the world of the text and that of the context in the process of meaning-making.

An Interpathic Approach

By the interpathic approach, I mean a method of reading both text and context with "the sensibilities of interpathy."[16] Interpathy is like empathy in the sense that both are ways to understand another through the imaginative projection of one's own feelings or emotional state onto the other. Yet in his book *Pastoral Counseling across Cultures*, David Augsburger makes a distinction between the two. According to him, with empathy people share common linguistic and cultural assumptions while interpathy is an attempt "to enter the other's world of assumptions, beliefs, and values and temporarily take them as one's own."[17] More precisely, interpathy is the process that "bracketing my own beliefs, I believe what the other believes, see as the other sees, and value what the other values, and feel the consequent feelings as the other feels them."[18] In this manner, interpathy is "the voluntary experiencing of a separate other without the reassuring epistemological floor of common cultural assumptions; it is the intellectual invasion and the emotional embracing of what is truly other."[19]

Based on this concept of interpathy, the sensibilities of interpathy mean the capacity to join others in their worlds. We become interpathic when we open ourselves to the otherness of the Other and are willing to change ourselves by the impact of otherness. This capacity involves two abilities: the ability to see as others see, and the ability to see ourselves as others see us. The sensibilities of interpathy make it possible for us to learn not only about the larger world but also about ourselves by looking at ourselves through the eyes of the other. Vulnerability and humility—not arrogance, aloofness, or fear—are prerequisites for entering into the other's feelings, life situations, and motives. By projecting one's own feelings or emotional state onto the other, interpathy builds bridges between different people with different identities.

One of the best ways to enter into interpathy with characters in a biblical text is to perform the text while preparing a sermon. This performance of the text involves experiencing the text through embodiment. In order to act out the text, the preacher must regard the text as a script and immerse herself in its world, playing the roles of the characters in the text in their own time and space. While Richard Ward, David Rhoads, Jana Childers, and other practitioners of biblical performance regard text performance as an event of preaching, I value the practice as a useful tool in preparing a sermon. By performing the text, the preacher can feel the text and interpathically identify herself with others in it.

Ward shares his experience of identifying himself with the Other while performing the text of the Syrophoenician woman (Mark 7:24–30) as follows:

> I remember that once when I was conducting a study of the Syrophoenician woman, my entire experience and understanding of the text changed when I physically assumed the role of the woman. In accordance with the "stage directions" given by the narrator, I "came and fell down at his feet." I realized that I had very little bodily memory of being in this kind of subservient role. As a white, North American male, I never had to "fall down" before anyone! By assuming the posture suggested by the story, I came to understand the perspective of others throughout time and history who have been oppressed by stronger and more authoritative figures.[20]

As Ward testifies, the performance of a text makes it possible for the preacher to feel the text interpathically, crossing the boundaries of gender, age, class, race, ethnicity, sexuality, and so forth. By embodying the text through physical motions and gestures, rather than through an intellectual play at a desk, the preacher experiences the text itself. Acting it out through physical movements also enables the preacher to envision others' thoughts and feelings from within a different culture, worldviews, and epistemology.

Though performing a text is an effective way to share the biblical story, it is not simply a matter of parroting the text, but is itself an interpretive method. As performance criticism explains, the performance of the text is an art of meaning-making. According to Rhoads, the text provides the basis for the performance, and at the same time, the performance gives life to the text. More precisely, the performance of a text is an experience of entering the world of the story, experiencing it, and reenacting it by retelling the story through imagination.[21] When retelling the story, says Rhoads, each line has its interpreted meaning:

> How you tell the story is . . . of utmost importance. . . . each line has the meaning content of its words, but when delivered orally it also has a subtext—the message that is conveyed by the "way" a line is delivered. Each decision made by the performer about the subtext leads to a change of inflection, the raising of an eyebrow, a distinct shift in posture, the lowering of the voice, and so on. In the text, there are explicit and implicit directions for choices about the use of these techniques in performance.[22]

Directions for performance implied in the text can be discovered by eclectically using such interpretive methods as textual criticism, narrative criticism, classical rhetorical criticism, sociocultural and historical criticism, and ideological criticism. Literary investigation into narrative by means of analyzing plot devices, conflicts, characters, temporal and geographical settings, narrator's point of view, and rhetorical style and techniques helps interpret the text in the course of telling the story. Historical and sociocultural criticism is also useful in analyzing the narrative world, especially the social locations of characters. Through critical analysis, characters can be identified by their cultural origin and worldview, social and economic status, family genealogy and kinship identification, gender and occupation, state of purity or defilement, health, education and religious allegiances, and so on.[23]

While this background information can be used as a tool to interpret the world of the text, ideological criticism can help the preacher understand power relations as the plot develops. There is no apolitical writing since all literature reveals the author's values and beliefs implicitly or explicitly. Ideology is "an integrated system of beliefs, assumptions, and values, not necessarily true or false, which reflects the needs and interests of a group or class at a particular time in history."[24] Ideological analysis discloses which values and beliefs the biblical text reinforces and which it seeks to subvert and replace. Ideological criticism leads the preacher to critically evaluate the text based on the following questions: What are the values and beliefs of the different characters? Whose interests are served by those beliefs and values and by the various characters' exercise of power? Who oppresses, and who is being oppressed, and how is the text served by this information?

The interpathic approach can be applied to reading both text and context. In order to interpathically understand Others who are different in their individual or group identities and social locations, the preacher needs to stand in their shoes and see the world through their eyes, just as she does with the characters in the text. This practice is not easy because such a reading requires the preacher to go beyond her comfort zone with vulnerability and humility. However, by transcending her boundaries with expectations of a new experience, the preacher can enter into a liminal space, a strange new world unfolded by the text and context. The preacher can practice the interpathic approach privately in her personal library or office while preparing a sermon. Yet a communitarian reading offers the preacher a more effective space for listening to other voices from both text and context.

A Communitarian Reading

A communitarian reading is to read a text in "a communitarian space."[25] A communitarian space means an interpretive community or "a hermeneutical space"[26] in which participants share their identities and life experiences when reading the text together. Rather than in the academy or in a lectionary group of clergy or in the preacher's private library, reading in a communitarian space is to read the text with a mixed group of people, composed of the cultural, ethnic, and gender diversity of laypeople and pastoral agents. A communitarian reading embraces an advocacy posture in solidarity with marginalized people and communities. By sharing the suffering and pain of others, participants read the text outside and beyond their own social locations.

A communitarian space should not be limited to church members but be open to the larger community, particularly to the Others of the dominant social group. These are the subjects for interpretation who represent their particular social contexts. They not only give witness to where God resides, what God is like, and what God's will is for their particular communities, but they also challenge one another to understand the boundaries of their respective worlds. In the communitarian space, the will of God in and for our globalized world can be discerned through a collaborative, creative, and global interpretation of the text. Considering that the Bible is the canon for the ongoing community of faith,[27] it is natural to find meaning in a communitarian space. By reading the text with others in a communitarian space regardless of gender, race, and class differences, the preacher can foster open, live conversation with others about a biblical text.

A concrete example of a communitarian space is a Bible study group. As John McClure suggests in his book *The Roundtable Pulpit: Where Leadership and Preaching Meet*, this Bible study group functions as a sort of "sermon brainstorming group (sermon roundtable)."[28] The Bible study group need not consist of only members of the preacher's congregation. Rather, it should include diverse individuals, both clergy members and laypeople. It can include more than the members of the church or the sermon-formation-and feedback group that I suggested for preaching as a team ministry in the previous chapter. In fact, it is much better to include people outside the church, even those who cannot take part in society, marginalized by gender, race, sexuality, socioeconomic status, and so forth.

Above all, during the Bible study time, some seats must be left vacant for some who cannot attend because of their geographical location, language barrier, and so on. When the preacher facilitates the Bible study, she or some members of the group can represent the voices of those who would occupy the vacant seats. For example, a white upper-middle-class European American congregation needs to hear how others, especially the socioeconomically and racially marginalized, read the same text. The preacher as a facilitator can reserve seats by placing some empty chairs in the circle of the group for the sake of the absentees. Then, during the study time, the preacher and/or other participants need to present the "absentee voices" based on their research or experience through direct or indirect contact with the Others. Like base communities in Latin America, a communitarian space makes it possible to engage in different voices of the community, especially the marginalized voices usually missing from society and the church. In this interpretive community, the text is read and discussed in relation to all the participants' experiences of God's nature and presence and activity in their particular contexts.

A communitarian reading presupposes that there is no single authoritative reading but only various readings by various readers based on their various life experiences and imagination. The basic approach to a communitarian reading is reader-response criticism in a communal setting. Although there are a variety of theories and practices in reader-response criticism, they commonly affirm that readers make meaning.[29] Reader-response criticism in a communal setting emphasizes a communal and social experience of reading rather than a personal and subjective one. By approaching "from below" and by critically reflecting on multiple readings from Others in a communal setting, the preacher tries to discern the word of God for the community in order to form a shared identity.

The process of a communal reading can be practiced in three stages: First, participants encounter the text for the first time without any assistance from scientific study. They read the text based on their imagination related to their previous life experiences and preknowledge of the text. Paul Ricoeur calls this beginning stage of reading "primitive naïveté,"[30] in which understanding the text heavily depends on the perspective of the preacher's prejudices. As Hans-Georg Gadamer explains, prejudice—a point of view from which one makes judgment—is a necessary condition for experiencing and understanding the world. Without a perspective or prejudices, we cannot begin to understand anything. However, it involves risks when participants bind the Bible within their inherited prejudices or use it as an ideological weapon to defend their own version of the status quo.[31]

The second stage of the interpretative process reduces these risks by reading the text critically. If the first stage is a sort of premodern reading, this critical reading is a practice of modern reading. The preacher provides the participants with useful information about the text: its literary and sociohistorical background. Through critical reading, the participants recognize differences between the social location of the text and that of their own lives. They also see their limitations and constraints in understanding the text. The participants' self-identity is revealed, formed in their particular social locations and circumstances; they feel vulnerable in going outside themselves to encounter the otherness and difference of the text.

Nevertheless, we should admit that even this stage of critical reading privileges some readings while silencing others based on the participants' points of view. In fact, no readings of the Bible are entirely free of ideological interpretation. All three—the text, readers who participate in a communitarian reading, and the preacher—have their own unique ideologies. Thus, one of the important tasks for the preacher in these stages is to discover a clue about "the power of ideology" or "the power of humanizing vision" from the text and, at the same time, shun the participants' conscious or unconscious support for "an ideology of power" or "the self-justifying defense and expansion of existing power."[32] When critically reading the text as the Other, the preacher should allow the text to expose and illumine the power of a humanizing vision, rather than permit the participants' prejudices or existing power of society to dominate the text.

The last stage of the interpretive process is to appreciate the text in our contemporary context. After experiencing the different world of the text, the participants then come back to themselves as if to another; the text is now open-ended to them with power to redefine their identity and reality. Returning to their own context, participants reconfigure the story, poem, symbol, or myth in the text with their creative imagination, emotions, and knowledge beyond the otherness and difference of the text. Ricoeur calls this stage a "second naïveté" in and through biblical criticism.[33] Freed from their social structure and fixed cultural ideas, the participants open themselves up to what is new in the text—new and different ways that the biblical text envisions—and actualize the text through a dialectical interplay between the world of the text and their contemporary world.

During this stage, the preacher can ask the participants to perform or retell the text based on their interpretation. Although the text is the same, their performances of it will vary, depending on their different interpretations as dictated by particular social locations and assumptions. For example, when I instructed students in my preaching class to perform the text of the Syrophoenician woman, a European American male student acted the role of the Syrophoenician woman like an aggressive person, even intimidating Jesus, while an African American woman played the same role as an assertive but polite and humble person. Consequently, their understandings of the gift of healing in the text were different. For the former, it was gained by the woman's aggressive attitude; for the latter, it was granted by Jesus graciously, who was moved and persuaded by the woman's wit.

In the communitarian space, the interpretive process is like a dialogue: a meaningful exchange between the text and the participants. Each dialogue partner, including the text itself, has power to influence others to shape their communities in a new way. The participants as others are not a blank slate to be filled, whereby their rights are derogated in the hierarchical structure or the relationship of dependency

between clergy and laity. Rather, they are to be regarded as equal partners of the preacher in a journey searching for the truth. Opening herself up to a genuine dialogue with the participants requires a certain
ethical responsibility of the preacher. Thus, in the process of dialogue,
the preacher must treat the participants with respect, listening to them
carefully and trying to avoid any misunderstanding. Likewise, each par-
ticipant also has a responsibility to treat the text and others with respect
by listening to them attentively and admitting that one's own perspective is limited and relative. Any intentional manipulation, fabrication,
misdirection of information, or misrepresentation of others' views is
unethical. Instead, real dialogue involves honesty, humility, and openness to different cultures and social locations at a roundtable in which
no positions are privileged and none are marginalized. This dynamic
interaction among different participants involves risk, the possibility of
being changed by encountering the text and others.

A Paradigmatic Interpretation

In transcontextual hermeneutics, the text no longer has a primary, single meaning but is best seen as discourse capable of creating multiple
meanings. When images, symbols, and stories in the text are read as
parables or paradigms, they have the capacity to develop into multiple
meanings. Parables and paradigms function as a way of looking at life
and of living it. Just as in the field of science a new paradigm leads sci-
entists to see the world of their research engagement differently,[34] so in
our daily lives a new paradigm leads us to see our world differently and
change our vision of a personal and corporate world.

Paradigm has a metaphorical character. Metaphor is not a mere
decorative ornament of speech but is a figurative word that includes
"a denotative or referential dimension, i.e., the power of redefining
reality."[35] In other words, the metaphorical character of biblical texts
makes it possible to create a new meaning apart from the grammati-
cal and syntactical facts representing its ancient cultural elements and
worldview. As metaphor, biblical stories, symbols, and images extend
their meanings to our world and reorient our lives by having referential
meaning as to how God is present and at work in our time. To interpret a biblical text as a paradigm means to see it as the clue that enables
the reader to have access to a new way of looking at the world by reading signs in both the Bible and our times. Rather than seeking a strict

analogy between the text and the context, the paradigmatic interpretation invites the preacher into a liminal space, a creative time in which she can engage in what the text is dreaming of to transform the life of her community and the larger world.

Reading the Bible as a paradigm is not a new idea. Contemporary theologians have stressed its significance for decades.[36] In his book *From Sacred Story to Sacred Text*, James Sanders claims that "the Bible, read as a paradigm of the verbs of God's activity, permits us to conjugate in our own contexts the verbs of God's continuing activity and how we may pursue, in our time, the integrity of truth."[37] According to Lehmann, a paradigmatic interpretation should involve not only the biblical story but also the human story. The human story established within the context of the new humanity has paradigmatic power, for such a story points to the humanizing activity of God in the same way that biblical stories point to God's graceful movement on behalf of creation.[38] Thus, in the paradigmatic interpretation, both biblical and human stories operate to help us envision God's promise and future hope as "a fragmentary foretaste of the fulfillment which is already on its way."[39]

A paradigmatic interpretation of the Bible can happen only through a dialectical conversation, the to-and-fro movement between text and context toward new meaning. The conversation is not a one-sided approach from text to context, or vice versa. Rather, it involves a reciprocal relationship where each is mutually dependent in order to produce a relevant new meaning for our contemporary time. As Gadamer explains, to conduct a dialectical conversation requires a disciplined skill to honestly consider the weight of another's opinion and bring out its real strength, rather than to look for the weakness of what is said and argue the person down.[40] To have such a dialectical conversation, the paradigmatic interpretation makes use of the interpathic approach and a communitarian reading. The dialectical conversation aids in discerning the will of God in our times and points to a perspective and direction for humanization, transcending the otherness of a text.

The paradigmatic interpretation can be illustrated with Mark 2:13–22. When the preacher reads it paradigmatically, she is invited to a liminal space, to Jesus' dinner table. The dinner table prepared by the tax collector Levi symbolizes an unusual space in which religiously and socially marginalized others share food with Jesus and other righteous people (vv. 13–17). The preacher who enters into this liminal space would be shocked by Jesus' radical acts and words. To the preacher, overwhelmed by this radical paradigm for a community in which people have different identities, the second story (vv. 18–22) affirms the power of this paradigmatic community by making a comparison to a wedding banquet. The guests whom the bridegroom invites to the inclusive wedding banquet discern the times and choose to disregard the old business-as-usual lifestyle of habitually observing such traditional religious practices as fasting. The text metaphorically illustrates the transforming power of this paradigmatic community with a piece of new cloth, not yet shrunk but sewn onto an old cloak, and with new wine which would burst the old wineskins and ruin them.

The preacher who reads the text paradigmatically is challenged to convey the transforming power of the biblical paradigm to a contemporary context. For Jesus, there are no boundaries between insiders and outsiders because God's grace and mercy are not limited to righteous insiders but rather are extended to outsiders marginalized as sinners in society. By freely crossing boundaries between inside and outside the community, Jesus reveals the presence and work of God's Spirit, which makes the human community whole. Then, how about us? In addition to the preacher's particular experience and knowledge, a communitarian reading will help her relate paradigmatic stories to our world. The preacher's task is to bring about the paradigm shift, a shift from the old lifestyle to the new one envisioned in the text, and then to her congregational life. The biblical paradigm will function differently for a community that regards itself as a group of insiders, righteous before God and others, than it will for a community that regards itself as outsiders, marginalized religiously and socially, or for a community that is struggling to cross boundaries of race, gender, class, and sexuality.[41]

A paradigmatic interpretation can also be applied to Mark 2:23–3:6. The text is about the serious confrontation between Jesus and the Pharisees over the observance of the Sabbath. When read paradigmatically, its referential meaning implies larger issues concerning our practice of the law rather than simply concerning the observance of the Sabbath in ancient Jewish society. Human history shows that laws have supported the vested interests of certain privileged groups, particularly when dealing with legal issues such as slavery, women's rights, wars, racial conflicts, sexual orientation, and the global economy. Contemporary people living in an age of globalization face a variety of legal issues deeply related to their everyday lives, emerging from the globalized economy and neoliberalism, postcolonial militarism, the dehumanization of immigrants and migrant workers, and various ecological crises. A few examples of such global legal issues include immigration laws of industrialized countries that ignore the human rights of immigrants and migrant workers; international loans and monetary laws that deprive developing countries of governmental sovereignty; and patent laws for water, food, clean air, and genetic resources that support a monopoly of transnational corporations.[42]

The text describing Jesus' deep compassion for the victims of the law provides us with a paradigm in which we can see our world through God's eyes and help the congregation connect with those who are underprivileged and victimized by a particular law. Through an interpathic approach in a communitarian reading, the preacher can communicate the suffering and pain of those who are different in race, gender, class, and so on. During the process of paradigmatic interpretation, a shared identity, a new humanity in solidarity with others, is formed, and a conversational fusion of horizons happens. Through such encounters, new meanings can emerge, meanings that might otherwise never be revealed.

Therefore, paradigmatic interpretation makes it possible for the preacher to read the text through and beyond its otherness by crossing the boundaries between the study of ancient texts and the study of contemporary life. This exercise is obviously interdisciplinary, requiring of the preacher fresh imagination and creativity as well as sociohistorical information about both text and context and literary knowledge of the text. Moving between text and context is creative work that enriches the life of the community of faith, giving it new meaning and nourishing it with a powerful humanizing vision. The biblical text as parable or paradigm functions to guide, nurture, and reform the life of the believers by providing them with a lens through which they see the world differently.

TRANSCONTEXTUAL HERMENEUTICS AS A POLITICAL ACT

For several reasons, transcontextual hermeneutics that reads the text by means of an interpathic approach, a communitarian reading, and a paradigmatic interpretation is in essence a political act. First of all, it is sensitive to power dynamics among different readers. Every reader—not only ordinary readers but also experts like a trained preacher—has a particular identity and experience in relation to that person's gender, age, race, nationality, sexuality, social status, and so forth. While this particularity presents possibilities for seeing the text from unique perspectives and enriches dialogue with others, it can also limit the reading of the text. It is noteworthy that Rhoads, when performing the Gospel of Mark, confesses his limitations as a white male performer belonging to the privileged class in society: "My social location makes it difficult for me to convey these marginalized positions from which Mark's Gospel was written."[43]

Like Rhoads, all readers have their own conflicts and limitations when interpreting the message of a text. It is impossible to interpret the text completely objectively or apolitically. What the preacher can do is be aware of the politics of biblical interpretation and think and act freely in terms of relationships of power. However, if the meaning of a biblical text is so exclusively determined by the social and political location of the preacher and of some privileged people in the reading group, judgments of truth or the discernment of God's will may never be made. With regard to this problem, it is important to remember that deriving meaning from a text depends decisively on the preacher. She is the one who controls the power dynamics of the conversation in a communitarian space and sorts it out to make an intentional and responsible determination when selecting the one meaning to apply to contemporary life.

Every reading, even if it uses egalitarian and democratic approaches, is contextualized, and different readers of biblical texts stand in asymmetrical relationships concerning power and their ability to speak about the text. Whose voice, then, is heard and valued in a communitarian reading? Whose interpretation among different interpretive voices will the preacher adopt in her sermon?

These questions are deeply related to the theological commitment of the preacher, which is the second reason why the nature of transcontextual hermeneutics is political. The preacher's theological commitment is not free of her political, moral, and social prejudices. Actually, the preacher's social location is decisive in how she sees the world, constructs reality, and interprets biblical texts. So it is necessary for the preacher to ask herself how her interpretation is conditioned by her social location and how it serves a political function. Even deciding on a meaning for preaching is profoundly related to the commitment the preacher makes, the commitment to our community, our society, and our world.

Based on theological reflection about the concrete questions and concerns emerging from globalization, the preacher needs to hear the Word of God from the perspective of humanization. The theology of humanization explored in the previous chapter confirms that solidarity should serve as a key criterion when the preacher assesses various meanings of the text. As Sharon Welch describes it, "Solidarity itself means a particular kind of action, a lifestyle expressive of sympathy for and identification with the victimized."[44] Welch warns that solidarity may be impossible, for "full empathy with the suffering of all people would surely lead to insanity, to the collapse of all conventional structures of meaning."[45] Yet the commitment to solidarity directs biblical interpretation to be an active struggle where practical possibilities can be imagined. Solidarity with others who are oppressed and marginalized provides not merely a theory for hermeneutics but also an impetus for political action, for constructive work for the global community.

The last reason why transcontextual hermeneutics is a political act is that it requires the public character of someone who has a preacher's sense of political responsibility and ethical accountability. The ultimate responsibility for creating impact through interpretation—whether or not it contributes to making and keeping human life human in the world—belongs to the preacher. The preacher is called to be a politician, to pay special attention to relationships of power, agency, and structure in a particular interpretive community, and to bring a radical transformation to the community of faith and eventually to the larger world. To fulfill this task, the preacher needs to ask herself how a selected meaning will mold the future of a world in crisis—a world divided between rich and poor, oppressor and oppressed, powerful and powerless—and what vision is produced through imagining the practical possibilities. Keeping these questions in mind, the preacher can discern what political interests are spurred by the very existence of an interpretive community, and then evaluate them critically by asking, What is the existing ideology of the community? How does that ideology contribute to a vision for humanization and a commitment to that vision?

Transcontextual hermeneutics as a political act can result in dissent or debates among the listeners, just as other political speeches do. However, when it is done in a theologically creative and rhetorically sensitive way, it can contribute to nurturing congregational apperception. David Lochhead shares his marvelous experience of a Bible study with Lehmann, in which the biblical texts are interpreted paradigmatically and the interpretation itself functions as a political act:

> Recently, in a small seminar of Canadian pastors, the American theologian Paul Lehmann dealt with two passages of scripture. . . .

The passages discussed by Dr. Lehmann were Genesis 13:1–13 and Matthew 25:31–46. The first passage deals with Abraham and Lot dividing the land between them. Lot chooses the valley land towards Sodom while Abraham is left with the hill country to the west. Dr. Lehmann pointed out that Abraham and Lot were coming from the south, and therefore, in turning to the east, Lot was turning to the *right*. To the right lies Sodom, which Dr. Lehmann interpreted as the symbol of organized dehumanization. In his discussion of Matthew 25, Dr. Lehmann repeated the familiar fact that those who were chosen by the King—those at his right hand—are those who unknowingly have ministered to the poor and powerless. But then he appealed to the geometric fact that the right hand of God is the *left* hand of the world. Bringing both of these studies together, Dr. Lehmann proceeded to comment on the "correspondence between theological and political designations of left and right," that the sheep don't know they are sheep and the goats are sure they are not goats. . . . In short, to the right lies Sodom. To the left is where room is made in the world for the poor and powerless. . . . Lehmann avoided the traps . . . by confining the theological meaning of "left" to the movement to make room in the world for those whom Sodom would exclude. What emerges from Lehmann's analysis is a set of symbols which relate the Biblical texts to the contemporary ideological realities. The analysis is undoubtedly debatable. What it does show is the kind of creative insight and risk which must be involved in [interpretation], the kind of imaginativeness which cannot be programmed by a method.[46]

My interpretation of Luke 1:26–56, which is the basis of my sermon "Dear Mary and Elizabeth," is another example of transcontextual hermeneutics as a political act. In the text, both Elizabeth and Mary have risky pregnancies. Elizabeth is physically too old to be pregnant, and Mary's out-of-wedlock pregnancy is socially and religiously dangerous, let alone unacceptable.[47] Nevertheless, the story depicts them as models of true discipleship by building a credible portrait of Mary and Elizabeth and showing how they respond to what they have seen and heard against their "shame-based peasant society" (vv. 26–45).[48]

The social location of Mary and Elizabeth was a poor, first-century colonized world in Judea under the Pax Romana, the Roman peace. The imperial monopoly of Roman rule exploited virtually all the colonized provinces. The colonized people were in poverty-stricken condition because of triple taxes being exacted for Rome, the local government, and the temple. They were oppressed not only economically but also politically and religiously, forced to show their religious and political loyalty to the Roman Empire. The cries of the oppressed and a thirst for peace in the colonized world were profound during the Pax Romana.[49]

I can easily imagine the colonized condition of Judea because I have heard how horrible it was from my parents, grandparents, and other Koreans who suffered such hardships under the Japanese occupation from 1910 to 1945. I consider Mary and Elizabeth to be resisters in solidarity with other oppressed people against the Pax Romana. They were energized by their faith to insist on the fulfillment of God's promises and demand the justice promised by life in God's creation. These two women remind me of some Korean female Christians who resisted against Japanese colonialism, imperialism, and militarism at the cost of their lives.[50]

Based on this understanding, I am determined to see Mary and Elizabeth as strong, passionate, and resolute revolutionaries who bring reform to their world, rather than to focus on their personal piety or understand their characters as stereotypically feminine: gentle, tender, and passive. My interpretation of these two women as revolutionaries is political in the sense that I intentionally choose the image of a revolutionary in order to encourage the listeners to follow in the footsteps of these women and to reform their dehumanized global world.

Mary's song (vv. 46–56) is not only an intellectually logical but also a heart-stirring depiction of a witness to God's politics. For me, it is a revolutionary song of humanization. The idea of reversal—the proud and powerful have been put down, and the lowly and humble have been exulted; the rich have been sent away empty, and the hungry have been filled (vv. 51–53)—is the political and ideological message for the oppressed and dehumanized in the world. Mary's prophecy in the song focuses on the heart of the messianic reign, in which normal values and expectations are overturned. Moreover, the rhetoric in the song evokes a revolutionary image. Mary's God acts not only for the powerless and oppressed but also against those who refuse to change themselves. God has removed those in power and replaced them with the lowly. As people in power change, the structure changes. Changes in the social order, then, will occur as leaders use their power to show mercy and nourish the hungry. As Vernon Robbins rightly points out, Mary's rhetoric is "a liberating strategy articulated at the liminal edge of identity to create the possibility for an emergent cultural identity."[51]

Who benefits by interpreting the text in this way? Whose ideology is being advanced? Definitely not the citizens of the Roman Empire! Not those who take advantage of the victims of suffering and oppression in a neocolonial or globalized world. The revolutionary interpretation of the text clearly stands for the poor, oppressed, marginalized, and the victims of post- and neocolonialism. The God of Mary and Elizabeth is the God of the Other. As a first-generation Asian American immigrant, I understand the hardships of immigrant and migrant life and see the Other in their communities. Analogically speaking, their problems and issues are in many respects like those of the people who lived a marginal life in first-century colonized Judea.

Christian believers living as a dominant group at the center of affluent society, satisfied with the status quo, will have difficulty in dealing with this shocking message, for it presents resistance against the established political and economic system. Nonetheless, there are surely some people at the center of affluent society who willingly relinquish their privileges and share their benefits with the other. There are some who, with the poor, the oppressed, and the marginalized, dream the dream of God's future and act to fulfill the messianic reign in our world, just as Elizabeth and Mary did thousands of years ago. The stories of their lives in solidarity with others function as a paradigm to help us discern the presence and power of God at work for humanization in, with, and under the concrete course of human events in a globalized world. Such stories contribute to the formation of a shared identity with Others: victims of globalization who are socially, culturally, economically marginalized.

Therefore, transcontextual hermeneutics as a political reading suggests to contemporary readers how to live their lives in today's world and how to reform negative globalism into a globalism of justice and peace. Transcontextual hermeneutics as a political act invites both preacher and listeners to be global thinkers by virtue of both *what* they think and *how* they think. The world, rather than just their local context, is their home. Global thinkers prize otherness and differences; they value views, assumptions, and preferences from an alternate life experience. Moreover, instead of immediate subjective feelings of evaluation, prejudice, threat, or defensiveness to otherness and differences, they feel a measure of inner freedom to discuss otherness and differences with a spirit of engagement and embrace. In this manner, global thinkers seek to discern the true and inclusive word and will of God in order to transform their communities and "to make and keep human life human in the world."[52]

5
Negotiating Diversity
The Rhetoric of Appeals

How the listeners listen to a sermon is as diverse as how different those individual listeners are from one another. Transcontextual preaching considers the diversity of the listening process as one of the most crucial homiletical issues. As some homileticians have researched,[1] each listener hears the same sermon differently. Differences in race, ethnicity, gender, age, theological orientation, sexual orientation, socioeconomic status, and so forth contribute to each listener's unique listening process, and further influence various modes of thinking, learning, communicating, and relating to others. With regard to language, people speaking a particular language see the world and understand its concepts differently from those speaking a different language. This opens the door to considerable misunderstanding when a person from one language enters a different culture and tries to adopt that culture's language. People from an authoritarian or hierarchical society are used to the top-down flow of communication, from higher to lower positions, while those from an egalitarian, democratic culture are accustomed to the mode of speech we might call discussion or talk, rather than commandment or order. Facing diversity in the listening process, preachers are challenged to reflect on their own ways of communication and seek new ways to think and talk about the truth.

It is unrealistic to try to accommodate every possible mode of communication into a sermon. How, then, can the preacher negotiate diversity without losing the substance of a sermon? What does it take to help the listeners move beyond their familiar listening processes and form a shared identity with others who are used to a different mode of communication? Transcontextual preaching takes this challenge seriously and considers it a matter of rhetoric. Although it is impossible to pin down a certain rhetorical style as the best communicative way for transcontextual preaching, a dialogue with rhetorical theories offers at least some homiletical insights into negotiating diversity in the process of listening.

Rhetoric originates in speech, and its primary product is a "speech act."[2] Rhetoric happens in a particular situation, which is "a complex of persons, events, objects and relations presenting an actual or potential exigence,"[3] "a situation under which an individual is called upon to make some response."[4] Classical rhetoric, rooted in the theories of Plato, Aristotle, and other ancient rhetoricians, was a systematic, academic discipline universally taught throughout the Roman Empire.[5] Rhetoric considers a speech act to be a creative work aiming to maximize the economy and beauty of discourse. For this goal, classical rhetoric provides instructions for the five categories of a speech: invention, arrangement, style, memory, and delivery.[6]

While foundational theories of classical rhetoric should not be forgotten or ignored, new contemporary approaches are worth noting. Rebecca S. Chopp emphasizes the significant function of rhetoric for community life, which lay outside the domain of classical rhetoric. According to her, rhetoric is "the art of deliberation,"[7] concerned with "determining life together in community."[8] Elisabeth Schüssler Fiorenza also takes into account the crucial impact of rhetoric on the life of community and stresses "an ethic of accountability."[9] To think about transcontextual preaching as a rhetorical act is to understand preaching in relation to its communal and public aspect of deliberation. Precisely, preaching is an art of public discourse, creating the space for the listeners to judge their basic understandings and values of life and consider possibilities from divergent points of view. Its theological direction should go toward humanization of the world, and every listener should be considered a potential subject or an agent for humanization.

In this chapter, I propose the rhetoric of appeals as the most effective communicative way to negotiate diversity in the listening process. The rhetoric of appeals provides necessary conditions for listeners to appreciate other ways of living and to be able to include that way in their corporate life. To create such a transformative space, the rhetoric of appeals provides the widest access possible by appealing to diverse listeners. This chapter will concentrate on exploring the rhetoric of appeals in three aspects: The rhetorical mode of appeals, the aesthetic dimension of preaching, and strategies for the rhetoric of appeals. The chapter will conclude with the image of a kaleidoscope as the metaphor of transcontextual preaching.

THE RHETORICAL MODE OF APPEALS

Classical rhetoric that aims at persuasion has traditionally dominated homiletical discussions. Aristotelian rhetoric, with its system linking ethos, pathos, and logos, is a direct mode of persuasion by logical arguments.[10] Because Aristotle's audience consisted of the upper-class citizens of ancient Greece, his rhetoric tended to approach this academic audience in an intellectually rigorous and complex way, involving "the systematic logic of deduction (reasoning from general principles to specific cases) and induction (reasoning from specific data to general conclusions), which followed highly elaborate rules and conditions."[11]

However, the listeners of transcontextual preaching are different from Aristotle's. Transcontextual preaching assumes an audience of ordinary people whose listening process is widely diverse. They experience diversity on a daily basis in a world of a globalized high-tech culture. They also experience in their daily lives such critical issues emerging from globalization as the unequal distribution of wealth, racial and cultural conflicts and discrimination, global destruction of the ecosystem, and the loss of a sense of community. These issues are too complex for the preacher to encompass in one forceful sermon. Yet we never know when an event of preaching may change a range of attitudes among the listeners and transform their social system. How desirable if this happened in the pews every Sunday! But as Anne Bishop reports, transformation in relation to these issues usually occurs gradually over a long term. Too brief or shallow an effort to change the congregation through persuasion without considering diverse perspectives among the listeners can trigger defensiveness or create a feeling of threat.[12]

To contemporary listeners, the rhetorical mode of appeals is more relevant than that of persuasion. Appeals are a mode of discourse through which we can engage difference in ways that are mutually challenging and dynamic. In everyday language, the term "appeal" has two significant common meanings. In the first definition, it suggests a kind of pleasing attraction. When we are drawn to something and find it attractive—a movie, music, dinner, house, clothes, or a person—we say, "That one appeals to me." In the second definition, an appeal means a petition or pleading. We plead or defer to the judgment of a higher authority, such as God or the Supreme Court, to render a ruling on our evidence, values, experience, or tradition.[13] Etymologically, pleading and pleasing are related to each other. In Old French, to plead (*pleider*) means "to agree" or "discuss," while to "please" (*plaisir*) means "to be agreeable." The Latin *placire* translates "to be acceptable, liked, or approved." The word "to please" is also related to the Latin term *placerne*, meaning "to soothe, quiet," or "to smooth, make even."[14] As M. Jimmie Killingsworth points out, all these derivations suggest interesting connotations for the word "appeal": "to be calm (as of the flat sea)."[15] "To appeal to an audience—whether to plead or to please—means to promote agreement or harmony, to smooth the waters between [speaker] and audience."[16] An appeal, whether in the sense of pleading or pleasing, implies "efforts to overcome oppositions and divisions either by forming new solidarities, by reinforcing old ones, or by revealing distances and likenesses in order to transform attitudinal conflicts into [communal forms of] action."[17] From these etymological roots, we can infer that the rhetoric of appeals is an art of communication that renders a message so attractive to an audience as to stimulate their minds and emotions to consider, and possibly accept, the idea of the speaker.

Like persuasion, an appeal is always directed to an audience in some sense. Yet the rhetoric of appeals employs an indirect approach. Killingsworth illustrates:

> When the poet says that the very skies cry out at an offense against the hero, we have an appeal to Nature that the ideal audience will find appealing. If an accused thief says, "As God is my witness, I did not do it," the appeal to the higher power is meant to sway the audience of police or jury. In these cases the appeal goes toward the audience by way of the third position, God or Nature.[18]

In this manner, the rhetoric of appeals proceeds toward its aim through stirring the audience's mind and spirit by appealing to something. Likewise, preaching based the rhetoric of appeals does not directly aim at persuading the listeners to conversion or transformation of their entire beings, but invites them to adjust their positions and to find affinity with someone who is different from themselves by invoking their imagination for a possibility of different reality. Therefore, the rhetoric of appeals is about working through differences rather than trying to make another person into someone like the preacher. Through appeals, preachers challenge the listener's deepest values and social structure and promote essential changes by "softening the heart of listeners and turning them to new ways of seeing, opening them to new ideas."[19]

Among homiletical resources, Augustine's work *On Christian Doctrine*, book 4, is valuable to engage in conversation with the rhetoric of appeals. Based on Ciceronian rhetoric, Augustine understands the function of Christian speeches in three ways, "to teach, to please, and to move,"[20] and categorizes them into three styles, the plain (to teach), the moderate (to please), and the grand (to move). According to Augustine, the plain style, using an unornamented language suited to factual statement or arguments, is effective for instruction or proof, while the grand style is used to move the audience with rhetorical modes of expression. The moderate style is between the two extremes—"more ornamented than the plain but less overpowering than the grand."[21] In this style, persuasion or consent is not a necessity, but what is said needs to be acknowledged as truthful.[22] For Augustine, both the plain and the moderate styles are auxiliary to the grand style because the goal of speech is to "move" or "persuade" the audience to implement what the speaker says in action.[23] To fulfill this goal, says Augustine, a single speech should not be rigidly limited to one of the three styles but be varied, incorporating all styles insofar as this may be done appropriately for persuasion during the course of the speech.[24]

Augustine's rhetorical theories give some insights into the rhetoric of appeals. Particularly, his advice of the eclectic use of all the three styles during the course of the speech is useful for the rhetoric of appeals. However, it is different from Augustine's in the sense that the rhetoric of appeals does not consider its goal the persuasion of the listeners to implement what the preacher says in action. If such persuasion happened by the rhetoric of appeals, it would be a grateful by-product, for the preacher who uses the rhetoric of appeals does not aim to win the listeners by a single speech but to appreciate their different perspectives and to invite them to a time for reflection. Thus, should the term persuasion by used for the rhetoric of appeals, it should mean "persuasion to consider."

Among many contemporary homileticians, Lucy Rose convinces us that the goal of preaching should not be persuasion. In her book *Sharing the Word: Preaching in the Roundtable Church*, Rose proposes "conversational preaching" as a radically shifted homiletical paradigm. She analyzes three different types of preaching practiced in the Christian church—traditional, kerygmatic, transformational—and criticizes them all for aiming to persuade through one-way communication based on a hierarchy from the preacher to the passively receiving listeners. According to Rose, persuasion should no longer be the purpose of preaching because it prevents the congregation from experiencing connection and solidarity in the process. Instead, Rose insists that preaching should be more like a personal conversation between preacher and congregation sitting at the roundtable. For her, preaching should be "grounded in solidarity—a shared identity as the believing people of God, a shared priesthood before God and within community, and shared tasks of discerning and proclaiming God's Word."[25] In conversational preaching, the preacher's role is not to persuade the congregation to her own view by providing answers or truths but to "foster communal 'reasoning together'"[26] by "[facilitating] the communal tasks of defining, maintaining, and reforming corporate identity and social order":[27]

> Conversational preaching in part grows out of and reflects the ongoing conversations between the preacher and members of the congregation in which the preacher is not the one-in-the-know but an equal colleague in matters of living and believing. Instead of impeding these conversations with a final or single answer, the preacher fosters them by explicitly acknowledging a variety of points of view, learning processes, interpretations, and life experiences.[28]

Just like conversational preaching, preaching based on the rhetoric of appeals is concerned with "mutuality, equality, connectedness, and intimacy"[29] with the listeners. In a world beset by conflicting attitudes and different views and values of life, it aims to open a window of hope for a more peaceful global community by inviting listeners to a deeper conversation, as part of the process of creating a community of solidarity. However, preaching based on the rhetoric of appeals is different from Rose's conversational preaching in how it attempts to create a community of solidarity. While Rose's conversational preaching offers a sermon to the listeners as a "proposal" or "wager,"[30] preaching based on the rhetoric of appeals is not merely concerned with offering a wager but also with attracting the listeners. How, then, can the preacher attract the listeners? By appealing to their aesthetic dimension. The rhetoric of appeals understands preaching as an aesthetic presentation appealing to the listeners. Through a beautiful presentation, preaching can attract the listeners to connect with different people by seeing difference as difference and by accepting difference not as a threat, but as an intriguing challenge to create alternatives to an unjust global world.

THE AESTHETIC DIMENSION OF PREACHING

An aesthetic is the key component of the rhetoric of appeals. While "aesthetics" refers to a branch of philosophy or art criticism dealing with the mind and emotions in relation to the sense of beauty,[31] "aesthetic" means an aspect of human experience pertaining to the appreciation of a sense of beauty.[32] When the term "aesthetic" is applied to preaching, it does not mean simply to feel things perceptible to the senses. Nor does it refer to a critical theory on evaluating the fine arts. Rather, it suggests the imaginative awareness of awesome wonder and an appreciative response to that. An aesthetic experience can be evoked by an immediate response to what is beautiful, leading the listeners to an appreciation of the infinite wonder of life. The rhetoric of appeals confirms that preaching can be the medium for such an experience of the beautiful.

Some Christians may be dismayed by the emphasis on the aesthetic experience of preaching and ask: Does it reduce the proclamation of the word of God to a human aesthetic experience? Edward Farley shares a similar reaction:

> Samuel Leuchli . . . asked a Swiss lay preacher visiting Chicago if he planned to visit the art museum. Leuchli records the reply. "Beautiful?" The man repeated incredulously. "Art museum?" He made a fist toward me: "I preach nothing but Jesus Christ crucified," he exclaimed.[33]

Beauty has never obtained the solid status of a central metaphor in Christian life, especially in the ministry of preaching. During the long history of the Christian church, beauty, on the one hand, has been an intrinsic part of Christian liturgy and celebratory festivals. On the other hand, controversies over Christian paintings, sculptures, and icons and the iconoclasm of Christians from other ethnic and religious communities reveal a dark suspicion of beauty in the formation of Christian faith. Moreover, some forms of Protestantism have opposed and criticized the arts—novels, dances, theater, and so on—for encouraging idleness and immorality.[34]

Farley analyzes three theological strands contributing to the tendency to suppress beauty in Christianity: the monotheistic revolution of Judaism, moral asceticism, and a dualistic worldview of apocalypticism. The monotheistic turn of Hebraic religion prompted the Hebrews to think of "deity as a single, personal law-giver rather than as a distributed set of powers of storm, wave, sun and mountain";[35] it stressed moral obedience to the one God without making any images of God, as instructed in the Ten Commandments. Moral asceticism practiced by monks and nuns through the ancient and medieval churches understood the self as unworthy of esteem, attention, or pleasurable experience. Even Protestant pietism understood true spirituality as sanctity that lives only from and for God, renouncing any aesthetic dimension of life. Moreover, according to the apocalyptic worldview, beauty is simply absent in this age, for the present world is ruled by darkness or evil power. "The beautiful new Jerusalem," then, is anticipated as a future reality; beauty as part of one's relation to God, nature, or other human beings is "apocalyptically postponed as an element of future salvation."[36]

In addition to Farley's three theological strands, our postmodern culture encourages some Christians today to disregard the aesthetic dimension of Christian life. Postmodernity tends to feature beauty in association with career success, physical health, and inner peace. Many magazines, gurus, television programs, and movements of North American popular religion express beauty in hedonistic terms. As a result, some contemporary Christians who are nurtured by moralistic, countercultural preaching react against this prevailing culture, and dissociate themselves and their faith from an appreciation of beauty.

However, it cannot be denied that the aesthetic dimension plays a significant role in human communication. It is also true that beauty has been a major concern in the fields of rhetoric, philosophy, and theology, deepening the relationship among God, nature, and humanity by an understanding of beauty. In summary, the concept of beauty can be seen in three ways: beauty as sublime, beauty as divine attribute, and beauty as experience.

Beauty as Sublime

"Sublime" relates to the ultimate experience of beauty; it is the appreciation of overwhelming greatness and beauty. Among classical rhetoricians, Longinus in the first century paid special attention to the majestic function of the sublime in rhetoric. According to him, when the sublime is expressed through a certain distinction and excellence, people experience not mere pleasure but a dimension of mystery and depth of the truth: "Sublimity flashing forth at the right moment scatters everything before it like a thunderbolt, and at once displays the power of the orator in all its plentitude."[37] Such an effect of the sublime is not persuasion, for it is beyond the orator's control. While the orator can control persuasion, she cannot effect the sublime.[38] However, Longinus asserts that the orator's efforts "to balance and blend inspiration" and her mastery of rhetorical skills and techniques can contribute to making the experience of the sublime occur.[39]

While Longinus limited the concept of the sublime to rhetoric, eighteenth- and nineteenth-century philosophers and theologians extended it to certain kinds of natural and supernatural experience. They expressed the experience of the sublime in such terms as "awe" or "wonder."[40] Immanuel Kant and John Dennis eschewed the reduction of the experience of the sublime to mere emotional feelings. Rather, they were convinced that through the feelings of the sublime, humans can passionately engage with the divine. According to Dennis, the primary object of the sublime is God, who is the ultimate mystery; and the experience of sublimity is an aesthetic bridge to the divine.[41] This view led Christian thinkers to relate the experience of the sublime to the experience of God.

Beauty as Divine Attribute

The eighteenth-century theologian Jonathan Edwards understood the nature of God aesthetically. According to him, beauty was not simply a human response to beautiful things, but it was "God's primary attribute."[42] The awesome creations of poets, sculptors, and musicians, said Edwards, were not beauty in its most authentic sense. Rather, the original and primary beauty was "the dispositions of benevolence to whatever exists," and an unrestricted benevolence was "the eternal loving consent that constitutes the triune being of God."[43] If primary beauty is heartfelt benevolence, beauty is not so much a feeling. It is not simply a human sensibility but a way of being engaged with the divine and with others in a community of benevolence and in the larger world. This aesthetic nature of God implies that God's self-revelation is itself beautiful and evokes joy and awe in the hearts of the people who grasp it. As Karl Barth states, God is "divinely beautiful, beautiful in His [sic] own way," and has "the power of attraction."[44]

Beauty as Experience

Beauty as God's attribute is revealed to human beings and can be appreciated by them. Thus, the location of beauty, or the place to look for it, is in human experience. Humans have the capacity to appreciate the beautiful not merely as an external feature but as an intrinsic element in the experience of their lives. In his book *Coming to: A Theology of Beauty*, William Dean affirms that human beings are aesthetic, imaginatively and responsively sensitive to the beautiful, with the ability to accept the world as a gift and to appreciate it.[45] Based on Whiteheadian philosophy, Dean claims that the aesthetic mode of existence is the "intrinsic value"[46] of religious life, for God is "the lure for beauty,"[47] and "faith is the state of openness to the aesthetically stimulating."[48] For Dean, intrinsic value means "the present satisfaction that makes life worth living,"[49] contained in some present event or experience. Thus, intrinsic value as a quality of satisfaction is itself the present experience of beauty. The experience is never boring, but a stimulating, awesome wonder.[50] The aesthetic experience, says Dean, comes when there is "a vivid contrast between the appearance and the reality." Here, "contrast" does not suggest a "contradiction," but rather a "divergence of a difference"[51] between appearance and reality. "Appearance" refers to the symbol for some different reality,[52] with its "symbolic reference"[53] guiding people to see reality from a different perspective.

The threefold concept of beauty as sublime, God's primary attribute, and experience leads us to realize the significance of the aesthetic dimension of preaching. Preaching has a revelatory character. That is, preaching is a medium for God's self-revelation, and the preacher is an artist or a designer who expresses God's beauty. Only beautiful preaching can reveal God's beauty (Pss. 27:4; 29:2). If the listeners appreciate the beauty—the benevolence—of God and then engage in relationship with God and with others who are in need at the moment of preaching, such preaching is beautiful. Beautiful preaching is itself an aesthetic experience, evoking feelings of joy, awe, and wonder:

> How beautiful upon the mountains
>   Are the feet of the messenger who announces peace,
> Who brings good news,
>   Who announces salvation,
>   Who says to Zion, "Your God reigns."
> Listen! Your sentinels lift up their voices,
>   together they sing for joy:

For in plain sight they see
    the return of the LORD to Zion.
Break forth together into singing,
    you ruins of Jerusalem;
For the LORD has comforted his people,
    he has redeemed Jerusalem.
The LORD has bared his holy arm
    before the eyes of all the nations;
and all the ends of the earth shall see
    the salvation of our God.
                    (Isa. 52:7–10)[54]

Preaching does not possess beauty itself, nor is it the location of beauty itself. But preaching possesses the potentiality of engendering actual beauty at the moment of preaching. This aesthetic dimension of preaching is not controllable because it stimulates fresh feelings "like a thunderbolt" through symbolic reference rather than through data-enabling sense perception or by the literal sense of words. More precisely, the preacher intentionally creates the symbol of seeing and hearing the world by means of stories and images, and then conveys symbolic reference to the listeners through her artistic skills. If the listeners grasp the symbolic reference and experience through it a new reality in awe and wonder at the very moment of preaching, it is an extraordinary experience because it is an experience of the Holy. We cannot expect that this kind of experience would happen to every listener with the same impact, for the experience of the Holy is always relative to the individual experiencing it. However, as Dean asserts, no experience of God should be considered "a solipsistic relativism, where no one shares what the other has,"[55] for the divine attribute—benevolence—is the primary beauty that transcends every relative experience of beauty. Therefore, any individual listener's experience of the Holy during the moment of preaching cannot be isolated from any other's.

The experience of the Holy has power to lead the listeners to appreciate life in an aesthetic way. By an aesthetic way, I mean a way of expressing an affirmation of life or the positive enjoyment of life, even with its negative aspects such as tension, chaos, and ambiguity. It is open to compassion, energy, delightful surprise, and unexpected gifts of life as well as conflict, suffering, and criticism. Just as "appeal" means "to smooth the waters" between the speaker and the audience, so preaching as an aesthetic experience smoothes the turbulent waters of communal and individual failure, limitations, and mistakes within the listeners, through the power of beauty—vitality, joy, creativity, and integrity.

Therefore, transcontextual preaching is an aesthetic experience that embodies both the pain and joy of life. Its rhetorical goal is to appeal to the listeners' aesthetic feelings by presenting divine beauty, so that they may be stimulated to live an aesthetic way of life.

STRATEGIES FOR THE RHETORIC OF APPEALS

In order to appeal to the listeners, the preacher must preach an appealing sermon, one so beautiful that it can evoke their joy, pleasure, awe, and wonder. How can preaching be such a beautiful experience? Which strategies are effective for the rhetoric of appeals?

Within classical rhetoric, Longinus's *On the Sublime* deals with the issue of how rhetorical strategies can create a speech that lifts the audience to the experience of sublimity. According to him, the key components of effective speaking are the quality and passion of the speaker, the due formation of figures of speech, noble diction in delivery, and dignified and elevated composition.[56] Though to some extent this instruction has timeless value for preachers, contemporary preachers must remember that our listeners live in a different milieu of communications from that of the ancient Greco-Roman world. Our listeners are surrounded by numerous communication technologies. The popular mode of communication in a globalized world is essentially audiovisual, drawing on sensory experience.

Yet contemporary listeners who are accustomed to this mode of communication in their everyday lives are seeking spiritual fulfillment, rather than simply knowledge or an object of thought, in the religious communication they experience. When preaching to this audience, classical approaches to rhetoric are not sufficient. Rather, we should note Dean's dictum, "If there is a vivid contrast between the appearance and the reality, there is aesthetic experience."[57] This implies that if preaching is based on the rhetoric of appeals, it will help the listeners experience the beautiful through "a vivid contrast" between a new reality and their conventional way of thinking, value of life, and habits, and the result will be beautiful preaching. To make a vivid impression on audiovisually oriented people, the preacher should pay attention to three rhetorical aspects: angles, the triadic path of appeals, and language.

Angles

The idea of having "an angle" is fundamental in the rhetoric of appeals, for each angle creates a contrast or a different kind of appeal. What is an angle? David Buttrick explains it in comparison with a camera lens:

> In many ways, human consciousness is like a camera lens. We focus on a field of consciousness. We can back up, widen out, and take in much, or we can draw near, narrow down, and attend to matters in detail. With the use of "filters" we can "highlight" certain structures of meaning, leaving others in "background." In consciousness, we can even determine "composition" and choose "angles of vision." All of us, as we perceive life, can say "I am a camera." Today, we have instant cameras so that, after snapping a picture, we can see, at once, what we are seeing. We can, perhaps, understand language as a kind of instant-camera film, for quite often we discover what it is we are seeing by speaking. . . . We discover through speaking, almost as if language were a film aimed at reality by the camera lens of consciousness—a film which enables us through speaking to "see what we are seeing."[58]

Buttrick continues the analogy of a camera lens in relation to an angle in preaching:

> Think of film making. . . . Today, [movie] directors use a camera on a moving boom so that camera angles change, lenses widen or narrow down, distances vary, imitating the way in which we actually perceive reality. . . . With different lenses and shifting camera angles, film makers give us an awesome sense of the real. . . . Twentieth-century consciousness views the world from many different standpoints.[59]

Angles in preaching are either perspectives or points of view from which the preacher sees the topic of a sermon. Just as modern novels "dance around in many perspectives"[60] from different times and places, from different memories and experiences, by means of flashbacks and interior monologues, it is necessary for a sermon to include variable points of view in order to approach diversity among the listeners. Although Buttrick was convinced that twentieth-century consciousness viewed the world from many different angles, our twenty-first-century globalized world demands that the preacher view it from even more variable angles. Different angles can contribute to creating a contrast between what appears to be something new to the listeners and what exists as the reality they are accustomed to. Various scenes illumined by different angles can result in "vivid" contrasts as we move from one scene to another.

The Triadic Path of Appeals

The preacher may ask: Of so many possible angles within one topic, how many angles—and which ones—should the preacher employ in one sermon? How can the preacher coordinate different angles to create a desired contrast? In relation to these questions, we observe that appeals follow "a triadic path"[61] in three positions: the preacher's, the listener's, and value's. The preacher's position is not simply her personal account. The preacher is a complex individual who selectively reveals aspects of character pertinent to the rhetorical situation. The preacher's position also represents a particular communal outlook that points toward a position of value and invites the listeners to join the community. The position of the listener may differ from that of the preacher, even if only slightly or temporarily, based on their sociocultural experiences. Therefore, the preacher must create alignment between her position and the listener's. The position of value, then, is "the triangulating point that defines (or re-establishes) the relationship," the common ground between the other two positions.[62] It is "the *ground* of the appeal, like the control tower of an airport, toward which the author moves and directs the flight of the [listeners] by relaying signals."[63] In many cases, new evidence and recognized authorities, or new experience and knowledge, are used as the foundation of the position of value.

A variety of approaches are available for the alignment of the three positions to create a vivid contrast. One is a direct appeal to the position of value that both the preacher and the listeners can readily agree on, regardless of their different positions. For example, when preaching on the issue of ecological crisis, if the position of value is that the earth is not a dead thing to be exploited and abused but a living being with which human beings share life, then both the preacher and the listeners may agree on this view, even though they have different positions on climate change. In this triadic path, the position of value is like a star that guides both preacher and listeners into the port of common interest and vision.

Another approach to the alignment of the triadic path is the use of a loose analogy between the position of the preacher and that of the listener. Precisely put, the preacher first relates her particular experience based on her own race, gender, social status, sexuality, and so forth as the conversation starter. Next, the preacher discovers in her seemingly unique experience a possibility of something to be related to universal human experience. She then invokes the listeners' memories of that experience that are similar to her own. Finally, the preacher appeals to the position of value established on the common ground of existential human experience. This approach can be applied to a personal story-telling preaching. For example, the preacher who is a first-generation female immigrant in the United States may have a unique life experience as a dislocated, powerless, and marginal person both at home and at work. But the preacher may find a clue to connect her unique experience to different listeners through research on contemporary human life. Her experience of dislocation, powerlessness, and victimization in society is in a sense a common human experience in some contexts and can function as the foundation for the position of value.

Determining the position of value requires that the preacher satisfy certain qualifications. Most of all, the preacher should be a practitioner of transcontextual hermeneutics. Transcontextual hermeneutics, explored in the previous chapter based on the interpathic approach, a communitarian reading, and the paradigmatic interpretation, provides a parameter for delimiting the numbers of angles and designing an effective triadic path. To use transcontextual hermeneutics effectively, the preacher, on the one hand, should be a diligent researcher. She must research the topic of a sermon broadly from many different angles through interdisciplinary studies in natural science, sociology, politics, economics, theology, congregational studies, anthropology, biblical studies, and so on. On the other hand, the preacher should have an ability to be attuned to the times, for transcontextual hermeneutics should never be done in a vacuum, but as a response to exigence. Exigence is "a sense of urgency, a problem that requires attention right now."[64] The preacher must catch exigence, prompting both the preacher and the listeners to engage in a certain topic and call the listeners to urgent theological reflection on that for the right moment. The urgency of the topic calls on the preacher to build the position of value as the need for change or growth, and calls on the listeners together to share that position of value—with its need for change and growth—with the preacher.

When the preacher shapes a triadic path for presenting the position of value, she needs to consider what kind of movement or logical development would effectively appeal to the listeners. Listeners have different anticipations when hearing the same sermon in the same place at the same time. The very intellectual listeners would prefer a communicative mode, presenting the position of value based on objective knowledge and accurate information. Those who listen to a sermon for a comment on life would like to hear the position of value in the mode of teaching moral wisdom. The very spiritual listeners who yearn for a mystical experience with the Divine would like the position of value to be presented as a clue for them to contemplate. Perhaps the logic of an argument based on the didactic style of syllogism and the mode of dispute may be helpful for the intellectual and moral listeners, while the mode of narrative would be appropriate for the spiritual listeners.

The preacher's dilemma is that in spite of the diversity of the listening process required for various listeners, the preacher must preach to them all simultaneously. One solution is to use a holistic approach that can appeal to all the listeners in some sense, though to different degrees. By the holistic approach, I mean the rhetorical mode of appealing to the point of agreement by stimulating not only human intellect but also emotion, intuition, and even gut feelings. The holistic approach is possible when the preacher is able to create a plot or a dynamic movement. Just as a scriptwriter drafts a plot in a drama or movie by employing sensory images and scenes, so a sermon should move from one scene to another with contrasting images, gradually approaching the aesthetic experience. Although the basic pattern of narrative plot is the movement from crisis to climax and to denouement,[65] many variations are possible, depending on the preacher's artistic ability. What kind of narrative plot the preacher can use for a single sermon depends on how the preacher wants to guide the listeners to reach the summit of the aesthetic experience.

Language

When creating a vivid contrast between appearance and reality, the design of the triadic path goes hand in hand with the use of language. While "conceptual language" provides human consciousness with "an abstract, limited, and fixed mental representation of reality,"[66] "symbolic language"[67] is pictorial and imaginative and thus leads not only the heads but also the hearts of the listeners. When the triadic path travels with symbolic language, it attracts and pleases the listeners, and eventually appeals to their entire being.

Symbolic language may be derived through intellectual learning or memorization of some beautiful expressions. But such learning remains at a superficial level. However, if the preacher draws symbolic language from direct or indirect experience, it will live together with her life and have a real impact. This is illustrated in the first homily (Exod. 16:1–3, 11–21) of my sermon "The Gift of Bread," which is included in this volume. In this homily I use the image of snowflakes, based on personal experience. The snow that I experienced in my dislocated situation was not ordinary but extraordinary, not merely a phenomenon of nature but also a symbol of the divine presence. With this symbolic imagery, I create a vivid contrast between a wilderness filled with emptiness and uncertainty and a wilderness covered with snowflakes—the manna—that symbolizes God's blessings in our everyday lives. In the second homily (Matt. 14:13–21) of the sermon, I use the image of a banquet, based on my experiences in attending various parties. A vivid contrast between a worldly, luxurious banquet "for members only" and one held in the wilderness for everyone, including the hungry, lonely, disoriented, and poor—this contrast appeals to the listeners aesthetically.

The preacher's distinctive delivery of these images and symbols through her unique voice further increases the listeners' aesthetic experiences, for the human voice, with its resonance and rhythms, adds aural impact to symbolic language. In other words, the preacher's voice is itself "an aural symbol." As Thomas Troeger states,

> The preacher's voice uses words and the physical properties of sound to draw people beyond the message that is being articulated into the presence of God. . . . It is rhythm and tonality of speech that carry listeners "far below the conscious levels of thought and feeling, invigorating every word; sinking to the most primitive and forgotten."[68]

Therefore, symbolic language conveys meaning by sound as well as words. The meaning created by language is intimately related to the "tonality of speech." The tone of speech is determined by the voice quality of the individual preacher. However, it is important to realize, too, that the preacher's tonality of speech is also shaped by her attitude toward both the listeners and the subject matter. Does the congregation feel attacked, condescended to, confused, cajoled, humored, imposed upon, invited, pampered, pandered to, blamed, or judged? The answer depends on what kind of tone the preacher uses. There is no formula for how to achieve a certain tone for preaching because "tone is context-dependent."[69] What worked last time may not work this time. Therefore, a general suggestion for creating an appropriate tone is only that when traveling the triadic path, the preacher should closely read the rhetorical situation and be flexible in responding to it with a contextually oriented tone.

TOWARD THE BEAUTY OF A KALEIDOSCOPE

In the field of cultural studies, some distinctive metaphors have been employed to describe different approaches to negotiating diversity in multicultural America. They include the melting pot, the salad bowl, and the mosaic. Each represents a different approach to addressing diversity with particular intentions. However, none can be the metaphor of transcontextual preaching because its way of negotiating diversity is aesthetic. It appeals to the beautiful in order to negotiate diversity. Appealing to the beautiful transcends the diversity of the listeners by stimulating their joy, awe, and wonder. Considering this aesthetic dimension of appeals, I propose the image of a kaleidoscope as the appropriate metaphor for transcontextual preaching. Before exploring this metaphor, a brief explanation of the other three—the melting pot, the salad bowl, and the mosaic—will help us understand the metaphor of a kaleidoscope.

The Melting Pot

From the early history of immigration, "the melting pot" was the prevalent image for America's approach to cultural diversity. The original intention behind this view was that "ethnic differences 'melted' into a single 'pot' would produce a synthesis—a new homogeneous culture that was not Anglo-Saxon, Jewish, Italian, nor Asian."[70] However, in reality, "what has happened in the melting pot conception of Americanization is that all varieties of ethnicities were melted into one pot, but the brew turned out to be Anglo-Saxon again."[71]

When applying this view to preaching, the preacher seeks the dominant cultural characteristics of the majority of the congregation and melts other marginalized subcultures into the pot of the dominant subculture. As a result, melting-pot preaching risks ignoring the diversity of the listeners. Rather than helping the congregants open themselves up to other cultures and engage in learning about one another to form a shared identity, melting-pot preaching maintains the congregational identity of the dominant congregational culture.

The Salad Bowl

An alternative to the melting-pot metaphor is "the salad bowl." In a salad bowl, "each ingredient in a tossed salad retains its own color, texture, taste, individual identity."[72] According to this view, in society like a salad bowl, "the sum total of all the ingredients becomes a multi-ingredient national identity without the individual parts losing their identity."[73] In reality, however, just as a salad dressing serves to weaken the distinctiveness of each ingredient by blending it with other ingredients, all thus acquiring the same flavor and taste, so the various members of multiethnic culture come together, blending their uniqueness with the dominant, controlling power of society.

The salad-bowl metaphor reminds us of evangelical preaching. Some evangelicals preach about racial and cultural unity with the hope of ending racial prejudice and inequality. According to their preaching, all who accept the evangelical orientation of faith and share that faith are sisters and brothers, regardless of their race and ethnicity. But the overwhelming push toward internal homogeneity by means of evangelical doctrines and dogmas is more likely to perpetuate the racial divide than to tear it down.[74] Rather than celebrating diversity, evangelical preaching suppresses diversity by inadvertently overwhelming identity issues with its salad dressing (e.g., evangelical doctrines and dogmas). Hence, the problem of salad-bowl preaching lies in the salad dressing. It relates to ideological questions: Who selects the salad dressing? What kind of salad dressing? What if some ingredients do not match well with that dressing?

The Mosaic

The metaphor of the mosaic has been favored by many theologians and sociologists as an appropriate paradigm for postmodern society. The mosaic—seen as a picture made of small colored pieces of inlaid stone, glass, and so forth—suggests an image of harmony and integrity of the whole, without any dominant centrality. According to this view, each community is like a piece of the mosaic. Just as all pieces are equally important in achieving overall harmony, different communities participate in revealing the wholeness of God by coexisting harmoniously with others.[75]

The metaphor of the mosaic seems relevant to presenting the diversity and harmony of multicultural society. When applying this view to preaching, mosaic preaching encourages preachers to listen to the voices of different communities, especially those of such marginalized people as racial and ethnic minorities, women, the poor, LGBTQ (lesbian, gay, bisexual, transgender, queer/questioning) persons, and people from developing countries, whose voices have often been ignored in the preaching event in mainline Protestant churches in the United States. Yet even here, the image of the mosaic cannot represent the creative dynamism of diversity. In other words, the whole picture of the mosaic is already framed by a specific design, and each piece is supposed to participate in completing the design of the picture with its particular shape and color. This static nature of the mosaic contradicts the dynamism of transcontextual preaching, which tries to go beyond the horizons of individuals and create beauty through dynamic mutual interaction. Considering this, the image of the mosaic cannot be the metaphor of transcontextual preaching.

The Kaleidoscope

In my book *Women Preaching: Theology and Practice of Preaching through the Ages*, I propose the image of a kaleidoscope as the viable metaphor for expressing the connectedness and diversity of women's experience.[76] This image is, indeed, also the most effective for transcontextual preaching. The term "kaleidoscope" combines three words in Greek: *kalos*, "beautiful" + *eidos*, "shape" + *skopein*, "to look."[77] It refers to a contoured optical instrument that illuminates beauty by a source of light. The kaleidoscope creates a multiplicity of symmetrical patterns from fragments of various materials, through the use of mirrors and lenses set at different angles. When the kaleidoscope rotates, each element produces beautiful, clear, and various patterns by its interaction with the others and with the light. Furthermore, when all of the pieces shift, tones seem somehow different in the altered positions, and we recognize the newness of the pattern.[78]

In relation to preaching, the image of a kaleidoscope represents not only the diversity of the listeners but also the dynamic interaction of different experiences among them toward their new shared identity. As Suchocki explains, when the kaleidoscope turns,

> not only do all of the pieces shift, but it even seems that some new ones have been added. There is familiarity and some continuity, for the colors are still there—but their tones seem somehow different in the altered positions, and while at first we try to see them in their familiar form, we nevertheless find ourselves struggling to express the difference in the way of seeing. Finally, we must recognize the newness of the pattern, and we reach toward a familiarity with the new that can be as assuring as that which we remember—or project—as belonging to the old. But the kaleidoscope will never repeat exactly the same pattern.[79]

Like the kaleidoscope that never repeats exactly the same pattern but constantly shifts to form a new pattern, kaleidoscopic preaching is open to inclusiveness and creativity. Moreover, just as a kaleidoscope needs a light to create a beautiful panoramic picture, kaleidoscopic preaching needs the source of light, God's benevolence, to illuminate the beauty of diversity.

One of the best examples of kaleidoscopic preaching is Martin Luther King Jr.'s "I Have a Dream" speech. It reflects the kaleidoscopic beauty with a sense of urgency by including a multiplicity of symmetrical fragments, different listeners who are King's Others. Jeffrey Murray accurately analyzes King's Others as including the following:

> First are those who have suffered oppression, those who have "come here out of great trials and tribulations." . . . King has heard the call of the Negro community. But King has also heard the calls of other Others and his rhetoric is responsive throughout. King addresses whites sympathetic with the Negro cause, welcoming those who "have come to realize that their freedom is inextricably bound to our freedom." . . . King addresses his critics and opponents, arguing that the "new militancy" threatens to "degenerate into physical violence." . . . [He speaks] against those who advocate "the tranquilizing drug of gradualism." . . . And King addresses those who are losing hope as a result of their suffering, urging them to "continue to work with the faith that unearned suffering is redemptive." . . . King's purpose is infused with the hopes and fears of his Others, . . . including his enemies.[80]

King's rhetoric not only is marked by the voices of numerous Others but also shifts toward the newness of their voices powerfully and beautifully at the end of the speech:

From every mountainside, let freedom ring, and when this happens,
. . . all of God's children, black men and white men, Jews and Gentiles, Protestants and Catholics, will be able to join hands and sing in
the words of the old Negro spiritual, "Free at last! Free at last! Thank
God Almighty, we are free at last!"[81]

All the sample sermons included in this volume illustrate kaleidoscopic preaching. For example, one is my sermon "Surprise, Surprise,
Within and Beyond the Church." In this sermon, I present a multiplicity of symmetrical fragments of life in a globalized world from
Korea through other Asian countries to the United States, as well as the
ancient Greco-Roman world. At its conclusion, the sermon beautifully
appeals to the listener for thoughtful reflection on the present situation
of their church and calls for their wise decision on choosing the right
direction for its future.

The possibility of creating the beauty of a kaleidoscope is based on
the preacher's multicultural competence and aesthetic sensitivity. To
nurture her multicultural competence, the preacher needs to have a
cosmopolitan personality. The preacher must increase her general and
specific knowledge about other cultures and develop the skills needed
to function appropriately in varying cultural contexts. Taking intentional steps to relate to racially and culturally different Others is crucial
for the formation of the cosmopolitan personality. For example, getting
acquainted with publications in racially and cultural different communities and developing educational opportunities to learn about their
history and stories are essential. In addition, pulpit exchanges, visits to
different racial churches, learning their languages, and joint leadership
programs across ethnic and racial lines both within and across denominations will provide preachers with opportunities to know about others
and to see their visions of community and global well-being.

If the preacher wants to present visions for the global community in
a beautiful way, aesthetic sensitivity is a prerequisite. Can the preacher
increase her aesthetic sensitivity? We assume that aesthetic sensitivity is generic. However, what Troeger says about the imagination is
noteworthy:

Yes, we can learn to be more imaginative. The imagination is not
purely capricious. If we analyze those moments of inspiration when
our hearts and minds take fire, we discover that there are patterns of
experience and reflection that encourage the imagination. Its activity is not random and chaotic. The imagination has principles of its

own. . . . The imaginative process can be compared to the art of sailing a boat: We cannot make a wind blow, but we can trim the sails and trend the helm. We cannot compel the Spirit to fill our imaginations with wind and fire, but we can practice those disciplines to open us to God's revelations.[82]

As with the imagination, there are patterns of experience and reflection that encourage aesthetic sensitivity. As with the imagination, aesthetic sensitivity can be increased by such effort and disciplines as close and critical observation of objects, nature, and human relations; creative and imaginative visualization of what we see, hear, and smell; visionary and integrative capacities of the mind to contrast between appearance and reality; and the inspiring articulation of the contrast in association with biblical and theological understanding.

With multicultural competence and aesthetic sensitivity, the preacher can create kaleidoscopic beauty. Because beautiful preaching does not refer merely to the wrapping affecting the external form but also includes the substance, the beauty of God, at the center of its presentation, the listeners can appreciate warm, personal loving-kindness and the compassion of God through beautiful preaching. Its ultimate goal is to connect the human spirit to the divine Spirit, enabling us to live by building affinity and solidarity with others.

Therefore, transcontextual preaching, like the beauty of a kaleidoscope, is an aesthetic experience. It creates the beauty of an identity shared with others in the Spirit of God. By appealing to the listeners for sharing Others' suffering and pain and imagining a common vision of a global future, transcontextual preaching moves us beyond our horizons to the beauty of a kaleidoscope, in the presence and power of the Spirit. Through transcontextual preaching, we are called to be beautiful and benevolent to others, just as God is beautiful for us.

SERMONS

Remembering the Gift of God

Ephesians 2:11–22

This sermon was preached in the chapel of the Iliff School of Theology. At the time, Iliff was going through some turmoil caused by an incident of racial discrimination, and all the constituencies, including the faculty, the students, and the board of trustees, were taking diversity training. In the sermon, diversity is interpreted as a gift of God, which is granted to us in Christ Jesus. The text functions as the position of value to which the preacher appeals. My southern white male colleague and I preached this sermon together as dialogue partners, alternating the moves of the sermon. We shared a variety of our experiences regarding diversity in race, ethnicity, culture, sexuality, and so forth, going back and forth between first-century cosmopolitan Asia Minor and different parts of our contemporary world. Through these multiple angles, the sermon transcends its locality and creates a vivid contrast between the appearance claimed in the biblical text and our reality in an age of globalization. The contrast is expressed in images of various sounds, generating sensory effects on the listeners' aesthetic dimension and stimulating them to envision a beautiful, new image of the joyful sound of building a household of God.

THE TEXT

So then, remember that at one time you Gentiles by birth, called "the uncircumcision" by those who are called "the circumcision"—a physical circumcision made in the flesh by human hands—remember that you were at that time without Christ, being aliens from the commonwealth of Israel, and strangers to the covenants of promise, having no hope and without God in the world. But now in Christ Jesus you who once were far off have been brought near by the blood of Christ. For he is our peace; in his flesh he has made both groups into one and has broken down the dividing wall, that is, the hostility between us. He has abolished the law with its commandments and ordinances, that he might create in himself one new humanity in place of the two, thus making peace, and might reconcile both groups to God in one body through the cross, thus putting to death that hostility through it. So he came and proclaimed peace to you who were far off and peace to those who were near; for through him both of us have access in one Spirit to the Father. So then you are no longer strangers and aliens, but you are citizens with the saints and also members of the household of God, built upon the foundation of the apostles and prophets, with Christ Jesus himself as the cornerstone. In him the whole structure is joined together and grows into a holy temple in the Lord; in whom you also are built together spiritually into a dwelling place for God.

(Eph. 2:11–22)

SERMON

PREACHER 1.   When I remember my teenage years,
one of my most joyful memories was
visiting my church after school
by myself,
which was walking distance from my home.
During the weekdays,
at twilight,
no one usually was in the sanctuary.
Whenever I opened the sanctuary door,
I could feel holiness in the sheer silence
and was led to pray amid the holiness.
When I grew up, however,
I learned
that the church is not always a quiet, holy place.
Rather, it has been full of a variety of sounds:
sometimes the joyful sounds of praise, thanksgiving, and laughing,
sometimes the jangling sounds of arguing and complaining,
and even the minor-key sounds of sighing and weeping.

. . .

PREACHER 2.   If you have a chance
to carefully read the Letter to the Ephesians,
you may be able to hear
the distinctive sound from the churches
in Asia Minor,
thousands of years ago.
What kind of sounds do you hear?
Since the first Christian church was born in Jerusalem,
the church spread from house to house—
from the households of Galilee and Jericho
to those of Damascus, Philippi, Thessalonica, Corinth, and Ephesus.
By the end of the first century,
there existed fledgling Christian churches
in all the cities in Asia Minor.
These Christian groups first began
among the Jews from the synagogues
in Jewish immigrant communities,
and later, Gentiles joined them.
Early Jewish Christians worshiped God in Jesus Christ
as one race,
with one tradition,
with the joyful sounds of praise and thanksgiving.
However,
these joyful sounds did not last long.
When the Gentiles began joining the church,
the Jewish Christians had troubles with them
because the newcomers were very different
in their racial backgrounds and religious traditions
as well as their languages,
dress codes,
and manners of communicating.
Moreover, they ate different foods,
even "stinky" pork,
which was prohibited under Moses' law.
No commonality existed
between the old Jewish members and the Gentile newcomers!

. . .

PREACHER 1.   Isn't it hard to live with people
who are different
ethnically, culturally, and religiously?
What kind of strategies could be used for diversity?

. . .

PREACHER 2.   The Letter to the Ephesians reveals that
churches in Asia Minor
adopted a policy of discrimination:
Jewish Christians were insiders,
and Gentile Christians were outsiders.
Jewish Christians were real members of the church,
and Gentile Christians were strangers.
Eventually
this policy of discrimination replaced
the joyful sounds of the church
with the disturbing noises of hammering and sawing,
for the church began to build walls
to divide the two groups,
Jews and Gentiles,
citizens and aliens,
members of the church and strangers.

. . .

PREACHER 1.   Well, I think
that we should not blame
the churches in Asia Minor
for their policy of discrimination,
because even for us,
diversity is not an easy topic.
Like the early Christians in Asia Minor,
we easily feel uncomfortable by those
who have a different color of skin,
or a different sexuality,
or a different accent in English,
or by those who speak a different language
or live a different lifestyle.
Naturally,
we humans seem to have hostile biases
toward people we consider "different,"
and try to build walls,
consciously or unconsciously,
to separate ourselves from them,
to protect our vested interests and privileges,
rather than share them with "different" people.
In fact,
we hear similar noises of hammering and sawing
as we build dividing walls
even in our own churches and schools.
Have you ever heard these kinds of sounds?

. . .

PREACHER 2.   I think I have.
Not so long ago in my hometown
in the deep South,
while the preachers in the white churches were proclaiming
in the pulpit that
"there is no longer Jew or Greek,
there is no longer slave or free,
there is no longer male and female;
for all of you are one in Christ Jesus" (Gal. 3:28),
the ushers at the church doors were instructed
not to allow people of color to enter the place of worship.
PREACHER 1.   I also heard a noise of hammering and sawing.
A couple of years ago,
one of my Korean friends,
who is a professor at San Francisco Theological Seminary,
spent his sabbatical with his family in England.
On one of his first Sundays in England,
they visited a mainstream white church nearby
and were happy with the worship.
His teenage son especially liked that church
because of its contemporary worship style.
However,
when they went to the fellowship room after the service,
no one came up to speak to them.
On the second Sunday,
they experienced the same cold reception.
The third Sunday was the same.
Finally, on the way home, his son said, sighing,
"Dad, let's not go to that church anymore.
They don't like us.
I don't want to be treated like an alien any longer."
PREACHER 2.   I hear the noise of hammering and sawing
even in our schools and churches.
Racial discrimination still is at work
in the very institutions that give us life.
PREACHER 1.   We also hear the noise of hammering and sawing
in our denominations.
Councils and conventions decide to build dividing walls
against those who are sexually different.
I wonder
how many churches and theological schools have truly tried
to stop making the disturbing sounds of hammering and sawing
and stop building the tall and strong dividing walls,
which safeguard the interests and privileges of

the dominant group of the church,
a group based on race, gender, sexuality, and class?

. . .

Perhaps some of us,
who are used to selfish individualism,
may ask,
"Why do we have to stop building the dividing walls
in our church? .
Why is it necessary for us to break down the walls at the seminary?
In our multiracial and multicultural society,
we cannot get along with everyone anyway,
so it's not bad to keep our own territory,
our comfort zone,
by building dividing walls, is it?"

. . .

PREACHER 2.   Remembering that
the ancient world of Asia Minor was
as multiracial and multicultural
as our world is today,
I guess,
even many churches in Asia Minor
would also have had no reason
to break down the dividing walls within their churches.
They might have built the walls
taller and stronger in their churches
in order to protect the comfort zone
for the dominant group.
However,
today's lesson from Ephesians
evidently tells us that
questioning the breaking down of walls is
anachronistic,
because the walls were already abolished in Jesus Christ.
No matter whether we like it or not,
the dividing walls between different people
were already broken down in Jesus Christ.
Therefore,
our hostility against different people,
caused by our natural prejudices
and a lack of knowledge of and experience with others,
is now powerless
because it was already overcome
through the death of Christ Jesus.

Our text reminds us that
we, who confess our faith in Christ,
are already in peace
with God and with others.
We are called to live in this peace,
not as the slaves of hostility
who rebuild the dividing walls
that were already completely abolished in Christ,
but as members of the household of God
who together build a new dwelling place
without the walls.

. . .

As most of us know,
Ephesians was circulated
among the churches in Asia Minor
and read at the services of worship.
The listeners included
Jewish Christians and Gentile Christians,
old members and newcomers,
male and female,
the rich and the poor.
I wonder what kind of sounds filled their churches
after hearing this letter.

PREACHER 1.   Well,
I can hear the whispering voices of the listeners,
voices full of surprise,
"Oh, that's right.
We forgot that.
We totally forgot the gift of God—
the peace—given among us. . . ."

What would happen, then, among those
who were reminded of the peace in Christ?

PREACHER 2.   I am sure that
those who are reminded of the gift of God
do not continue building walls.
Instead, they begin another construction site,
building a new dwelling place,
a "holy temple,"
where God resides with them.
In the new structure of this household of God,
there are no longer divisions

but a oneness in Christ Jesus—
forgiveness and reconciliation.
This new floor plan invites everyone
to participate in building the new household of God,
regardless of one's race, gender, sexuality, and class.

. . .

Can you imagine this new construction,
building together the household of God?
Can you see the faces of the builders,
full of smiles and amazement?

PREACHER 1.   I can see them hammering and sawing.
Yet this time
their hammering and sawing
does not make an uncomfortable chill, discordant noise
but a delightful rhythmic sound
with laughter and whistling,
to the melody of a harmonious and joyful song of peace.

. . .

Among the crowds of listeners
who have been invited to join the new construction,
I find *our* faces, *too*,
gathered in this room.

The Gift of Bread

Exodus 16:1–3, 11–21; Matthew 14:13–21

This sermon consists of a pair of homilies (or minisermons), one based on the Old Testament text and the other on the New Testament text. Between them, a song, "Panis Angelicus," by Cesar Franck, provides a moment of meditation in the course of preaching. These three parts of the sermon are integrated under one common theme presented by the sermon title, "The Gift of Bread." The gift of heavenly bread is seen from two points of view, personal in the first homily, communal in the second homily.

In the first homily, I share my personal experience of moving to a strange, new place, hoping that the listeners will remember their own personal experiences similar to mine and connect them with my story. The text provides the term "wilderness" as the metaphor connoting the locus of our living in a globalized world and leading me to interpret my personal experience of moving as a wilderness experience. Wilderness is presented in two contrasting images: the wilderness of hunger and loneliness, and the wilderness of wonder and awe. My experience with snowflakes in Colorado is compared to the Israelites' experience with manna in the wilderness and is described as an experience of sublimity. I preached this sermon to a local congregation in Denver, Colorado, and appealed to the listeners' aesthetic experience with the snow. By remembering snowflakes falling silently and abundantly, the listeners may feel the presence of God in their daily lives and be fed by the divine gift in their wilderness life.

121

Following the first homily, I take a short break, sitting in the preacher's chair at the chancel while "Panis Angelicus" is sung by a member of the congregation. After the song, I recite the New Testament text and preach the second homily. The second homily begins with a dialogue with the listeners and asks a question about a banquet. The image of a banquet serves as the key metaphor for the entire homily. The listeners are invited to experience a vivid contrast between the appearance, an extraordinary banquet held in the wilderness by Jesus, and the reality, an ordinary banquet experienced in our worldly lives. The beautiful nature of God described through the compassion of Jesus in the text appeals to the listeners by invoking a joyful response to the divine call for ethical responsibility of sharing their possessions with those who are variously in need: the lonely, the disoriented, and the poor in our globalized world.

To give the listeners a vivid picture of the wandering Israelites in the wilderness, I prepared the Scripture reading from the Old Testament as an "ensemble reading," dramatized by a group of people. Some church members were invited to participate in the ensemble reading by coming to the church thirty minutes early to practice it as a group before the service began.

THE OLD TESTAMENT TEXT: AN ENSEMBLE READING

Six Readers (a narrator, three choruses, the Lord, Moses)
(Note: Elim is pronounced *EE-lim.*)

NARRATOR.   The whole congregation of the Israelites set out from Elim; and Israel came to the wilderness of Sin, which is between Elim and Sinai, on the fifteenth day of the second month after they had departed from the land of Egypt.

NARRATOR.   The whole congregation of the Israelites complained against Moses and Aaron in the wilderness.

CHORUS 1.   If only we had died by the hand of the LORD in the land of Egypt,

CHORUS 2.   (*longingly*) when we sat by the fleshpots and ate our fill of bread;

CHORUS 3.   for you have brought us out into this wilderness to kill this whole assembly with hunger.
            (*general murmurs of discontent and outrage among the entire chorus*)

NARRATOR.	(*stopping the chorus's murmurs*) The LORD spoke to Moses and said,
THE LORD.	I have heard the complaining of the Israelites; say to them, "At twilight you shall eat meat, and in the morning you shall have your fill of bread; then you shall know that I am the LORD your God!"
NARRATOR.	In the evening quails came up and covered the camp; and in the morning there was a layer of dew around the camp. When the layer of dew lifted, there was a fine flaky substance, as fine as frost on the ground. When the Israelites saw it, they said to one another,
CHORUS 2.	What is it?
CHORUS 1.	(*in character*) For they did not know *what* it was!
NARRATOR.	Moses said to them,
MOSES.	It is the bread that the LORD has given you to eat. This is what the LORD has commanded:
THE LORD.	Gather as much of it as each of you needs, an omer to a person according to the number of persons, all providing for those in their own tents.
NARRATOR.	The Israelites did so,
CHORUS 3.	some gathering more,
CHORUS 1.	some gathering less.
NARRATOR.	But when they measured it with an omer,
CHORUS 3.	those who gathered much had nothing over,
CHORUS 1.	and those who gathered little had no shortage.
CHORUS 3 AND CHORUS I TOGETHER.	They gathered as much as each of them needed!
NARRATOR.	And Moses said to them,
MOSES.	Let no one leave any of it over until morning!
NARRATOR.	But they did not listen to Moses; some left part of it until morning,
CHORUS 2.	(*disgusted*) and it bred worms and became . . . foul!
MOSES.	(*with some heat*) I am angry with you!
NARRATOR.	Morning by morning they gathered it, as much as each needed; but when the sun grew hot,
CHORUS 2.	it melted.
NARRATOR.	Here ends the reading of the Old Testament. (adapted from Exod. 16:1–3, 11–21)[1]

HOMILY 1

I am sure
that many of you have experienced moving,
from one town to another,
or from state to state,
or from country to country.
Before my family and I moved to Denver,
we had lived in Princeton, New Jersey, for over twelve years.
I still have a vivid memory
Of when we first moved to Denver.

. . .

When I received a job offer from the Iliff School of Theology,
my husband and I were very excited
because we finally had a chance
to live in a different area of the United States.
When we told our friends that
we were moving to Colorado,
they envied us a lot by saying,
"Wow! Colorado!
You are lucky to get a job there.
I bet Colorado is one of the best places to live in the United States."
Well,
in spite of such encouraging words,
moving from the east coast out to the west was
quite a wild experience for my family.
You know, in my opinion,
moving is one of the most stressful events in life.
Five days after we arrived in Denver,
our huge moving truck arrived
and unloaded over one hundred boxes.
Unpacking them was very labor-intensive.
Even several weeks after our move,
we were still surrounded by boxes and more boxes.

. . .

One night, almost at midnight,
my husband and I were unpacking.
While working on this seemingly never-ending chore,
we didn't say word to each other.
There was a dry silence throughout the house
except for the sharp sound of opening boxes and intermittent sighs.
Maybe we didn't want to talk because we were physically tired.

Even looking at the piles of boxes exhausted us.
But there was another reason,
the real reason why we were silent.
Just as the Israelites felt hungry and thirsty
when they left Egypt and entered into a strange, new land of wilderness,
so our hearts too were filled with
emptiness and uncertainty.
Princeton had been our second hometown.
Since we immigrated from Korea,
we had lived only there.
We missed everything that we had left behind—
our friends, our church, Nassau Street, Carnegie Lake,
and the Thomas Sweet Ice Cream store.
Everything there was familiar to us.
But now we found ourselves in a strange land.
Were we going to be okay in this wilderness?
Would our new jobs be secure?
Would our new friends and neighbors be kind to us,
minority people?
Were we going to find a good church?
. . .
More directly speaking,
was God going to be with us even in this strange land?
Preoccupied with these anxieties,
I stopped unpacking and sat on a sofa in the living room.
When I happened to casually open the curtain,
I was amazed by the brightness outside.
Although it was midnight,
outside it was as bright as dawn.
When I looked out the window more closely,
something was falling from heaven.
"What is it?" I asked myself.
They were snowflakes!
All the outside world—
all the trees, rooftops, and roads were covered thickly by white snow.
I shouted to my husband,
"Honey, look out the window! It's snowing!"
Then, he said, "Snow in April?"
Yes, it was unbelievable for us to have snow in April
because back in Princeton, we had never experienced
a snowy day in April.
Of course, now we have learned that

it is pretty much a natural phenomenon
to have heavy snowfall in the foothills of the Rocky Mountains
even in May or even in June!
Amazed by the snowflakes,
my husband and I were enticed to open the porch door
and go out to the front yard.
We held hands and looked up at the sky.
The snow was falling silently
on our heads, our faces, and our shoulders.
My husband and I were in awe,
like the Israelites who were amazed
when they first saw the manna in the wilderness,
the layer of a white flaky substance,
covering the ground in great abundance.
The manna from heaven, the divine gift!
The snow melted our fears about our uncertain future
and filled our empty hearts with a renewed faith in God.
Feeling the divine presence through the snow,
I whispered to God,
"Thank you! Thank you, Lord!
You are with us even in this wilderness."
. . .
The wilderness was not a place of hunger or thirst for the Israelites.
God fed them with manna
over their forty years in the wilderness,
without want of anything.
Even for us, here and now,
the wilderness is not a place of loneliness or anxiety.
There is the gift of bread from heaven,
which enables us to have life, a new world, a new reality
even in our life of wilderness.
. . .
Can you see God's everyday blessings
in your daily lives, silent and abundant like snowflakes?

SPECIAL SONG

"Panis Angelicus," by Cesar Franck

THE NEW TESTAMENT TEXT

Now when Jesus heard this, he withdrew from there in a boat to a deserted place by himself. But when the crowds heard it, they followed him on foot from the towns. When he went ashore, he saw a great crowd; and he had compassion for them and cured their sick. When it was evening, the disciples came to him and said, "This is a deserted place, and the hour is now late; send the crowds away so that they may go into the villages and buy food for themselves." Jesus said to them, "They need not go away; you give them something to eat." They replied, "We have nothing here but five loaves and two fish." And he said, "Bring them here to me." Then he ordered the crowds to sit down on the grass. Taking the five loaves and the two fish, he looked up to heaven, and blessed and broke the loaves, and gave them to the disciples, and the disciples gave them to the crowds. And all ate and were filled; and they took up what was left over of the broken pieces, twelve baskets full. And those who ate were about five thousand men, besides women and children.

(Matthew 14:13–21)

HOMILY 2

I have a question:
Have you ever been to a banquet?
I do not mean a banquet like an ordinary dinner party
with your friends or family
at a decent restaurant;
I do not mean a banquet like a New Year's Eve party
for the wealthy "members only,"
in the fancy ballroom of a five-star hotel
with exquisite music and exotic food.
I mean a banquet
held in a deserted place at twilight,
serving thousands of people,
not only men and women but also little children.
Actually,
the people who are invited are the hungry and weary.
This party doesn't serve luxurious cooked dishes or expensive wine.
Rather, it serves an ordinary daily meal.
However,
the people are fully fed and satisfied with just enough food,
a joyful banquet in which everyone feels connected to one another.

. . .

Today's Gospel lesson tells us about this extraordinary banquet,
held in the wilderness near the shore of Galilee.
According to previous verses,
John the Baptist, who was the hope of the poor and weak,
was beheaded at a royal banquet,
which celebrated King Herod's birthday.
After hearing about the pride, arrogance, and murder
that happened at Herod's luxurious orgy,
Jesus was so disheartened
that he went to a deserted place to be by himself.
However,
a huge crowd followed him,
to listen to him, to touch him, and to be healed by him.
When Jesus saw this great crowd,
who were helpless like sheep without a shepherd,
he had compassion for them and cured their sicknesses.
And furthermore, he held a banquet to feed them.
How could Jesus feed them in this remote place
without food available?
In fact, his disciples suggested
that he should send the crowds away,
so they could go to the villages and buy some food.
Nevertheless,
instead of dismissing the crowds,
Jesus asked his disciples to bring to him what they had—
five loaves of bread and two fish.
When he took them, he gave thanks and broke the bread.
And when the disciples gave the broken bread to the people,
you know what happened!
In front of the disciples,
who were skeptical about their small supply of food,
five loaves and two fish
were multiplied to feed
five thousand men
plus women and children,
including twelve basketfuls of leftovers.

. . .

Through divine intervention,
five loaves and two fish were enough,
indeed more than enough for the disciples
to feed the huge crowds.
These meager resources were enough for Jesus
to prepare a joyful banquet in the wilderness.

The wilderness of hunger and thirst was turned into
a banquet place,
in which joy and satisfaction overflowed.

. . .

My dear friends,
Have you ever been in the wilderness?
What have you seen there?
I see the lonely, the disoriented, and the poor in many different ways.
I see the ones who are in despair over the loss of their loved ones;
I see the anxious faces of those who have lost their jobs;
I see a single mother and her little children,
whose lives depend on her minimum hourly wage.
I see new immigrants who are estranged because of racist attitudes.
I also see a friend who once desperately told me,
"I am tired of how I am treated because I am gay."
Perhaps it is impossible for us
to change the wilderness into a joyful banquet place,
where everyone is fed and satisfied with abundant food
because all that we have are
merely five loaves and two fish:
our time and energy,
and our knowledge and experience are limited;
even the churches that we serve have
only small numbers on the membership rolls
and even smaller numbers for the mission budget.
It would be no wonder, then,
if we joined the disciples in crying,
"This is a desert.
Send the crowds away to fend for themselves."

. . .

Yet,
we hear the voice of Jesus in the wilderness,
"Bring your five loaves of bread and two fish to me."
"Bring them here to me."

. . .

I believe we are the ones
Who must trust in the divine power and share our bread
to have Jesus work a miracle again,
so that everyone who is lonely, disoriented, and poor
may join in celebrating the heavenly banquet
by tasting the messianic meal together!
May the Word of God be fulfilled in your ministry!
Amen.

Surprise, Surprise, Within and Beyond the Church

Genesis 11:1–9; Romans 12:1–8

This sermon deals with the issue of racial and cultural diversity based on my experience of globalization both in Korea and in the United States. Moving between Korea and the United States and between the two biblical worlds of the Old and New Testament texts by sharing stories, the sermon addresses problems caused by diversity throughout human history and calls for critical reflection on them. Various scenes developed from multiple angles in the sermon connect the listeners with the present situation of racial and cultural diversity at church and in society. The sermon appeals to the listeners by stimulating their imagination for envisioning a beautiful, new world based on diversity. This sermon was originally preached at my own church; it motivated the congregation to develop a series of forums on racial issues, at which different ethnic leaders across denominations were invited to explore racial policies, immigration law, and the growth of multiracial churches.

The Old Testament text is prepared as an ensemble reading in order to employ different tones or voice effects when reciting the story, especially to highlight the word "scattered" in various tones. In the New Testament reading, the Greek term *charismata* is inserted in verse 6 to stress the significance of "grace-gift."

THE OLD TESTAMENT TEXT: AN ENSEMBLE READING

Three voices (Voice 1, Voice 2, Voice 3)

VOICE 1.	Now the whole earth had one language
ALL.	and the same words.
VOICE 2.	And as they migrated from the east, they came upon a plain in the land of Shinar and settled there.
VOICE 3.	And they said to one another, "Come, let us make bricks, and burn them thoroughly."
VOICE 2.	And they had brick for stone,
VOICE 1.	and bitumen for mortar.
ALL.	Then they said,
VOICE 2.	Come let us build ourselves a city,
VOICE 1.	and a tower with its top in the heavens,
VOICE 3.	and let us make a name for ourselves;
ALL.	otherwise
VOICE 3.	we shall be scattered abroad upon the face of the whole earth.
VOICE 1.	Scattered.
VOICE 2.	Scattered.
	(*pause*)
VOICE 2.	The LORD came down to see the city and the tower, which mortals had built. And the LORD said,
ALL.	Look,
VOICE 1.	they are one people, and they have all one language;
VOICE 2.	and this is only the beginning of what they will do;
VOICE 3.	nothing that they propose to do will now be impossible for them.
VOICE 1.	Come, let us go down,
VOICE 3.	and confuse their language there,
VOICE 2.	so that they will not understand one another's speech.
VOICE 1.	So the LORD scattered them abroad from there over the face of all the earth,
VOICE 3.	and they left off building the city.
VOICE 1.	Therefore it was called Babel, because there the LORD confused the language of all the earth;
VOICE 2.	and from there the LORD scattered them abroad over the face of all the earth.
VOICE 3.	Scattered.
VOICE 1.	Scattered.
ALL.	Scattered.
	(adapted from Gen. 11:1–9)[2]

THE NEW TESTAMENT TEXT

I appeal to you therefore, brothers and sisters, by the mercies of God, to present your bodies as a living sacrifice, holy and acceptable to God, which is your spiritual worship. Do not be conformed to this world, but be transformed by the renewing of your minds, so that you may discern what is the will of God—what is good and acceptable and perfect. For by the grace given to me I say to everyone among you not to think of yourself more highly than you ought to think, but to think with sober judgment, each according to the measure of faith that God has assigned. For as in one body we have many members, and not all the members have the same function, so we, who are many, are one body in Christ, and individually we are members one of another. We have gifts [*charismata*] that differ according to the grace given to us: prophecy, in proportion to faith; ministry, in ministering; the teacher, in teaching; the exhorter, in exhortation; the giver, in generosity; the leader, in diligence; the compassionate, in cheerfulness.

(Romans 12:1–8)

SERMON

This past year,
I returned to Korea, my native country,
which I had left twenty years before.
. . .
During my visit last fall,
I was continuously surprised
by changes in Korea.
And the greatest surprise was
that Korea was becoming a multiracial and multicultural society.
Traditionally,
Korea has been proud to be a homogeneous nation,
of one race and one language.
But now, this is simply history.
Every year
the influx of different ethnic people is increasing.
The land size of South Korea is
about one-third the size of the state of Colorado,
and its population is over forty-five million.
Today

more than half a million migrant workers are visible in such
a dense nation.
Most of them come from Asian and African countries,
to make money to support their families,
who are struggling to survive day by day in their homelands,
impoverished by injustice, inequality,
and the disparity wrought by a global economy.
Imagine the migrant workers' vulnerable lives
under biased sociopolitical and racial policies
and cultural discrimination in a foreign land.

. . .

While in Korea,
I visited various churches—
from megachurches in rich suburban areas,
to small churches on the margins of society.
And what a surprise to find
the impact of globalization even in the churches!
Many of them were facing the issue of
ethnic and cultural diversity,
which was absolutely unprecedented in Korean churches.
Considering that Korea has been a relatively monocultural society
and that Korean churches have traditionally been
homogeneous groups,
the issue of diversity should be very difficult
for them to tackle.
In fact,
many churches in Korea were traumatized
simply by the *fear* of diversity.
Diversity!
It is a serious global issue!
The fear of diversity is a global symptom!

. . .

Well, we must confess
that our American churches haven't had such a beautiful history
regarding racial, ethnic, and cultural diversity.
Since Martin Luther King Jr. reminded us
almost half a century ago
that Sunday mornings were the most segregated time
of the entire week in the United States,
we have not yet seen any radical changes.
Still, today, Euro-Americans like to flock together,
and African Americans, Hispanic Americans,
Korean and other Asian Americans are no exception.

Maybe it is a natural human proclivity to stay close to those
of the same ethnic and cultural backgrounds.
A Korean friend of mine,
who recently immigrated to the United States,
shared with me his first experience in the United States:
On his first Sunday in the United States,
he and his family visited a Euro-American church
near their new home.
After the service,
they went to the fellowship hall to chat with others.
The pastor came up to my friend,
took him outside the church building,
and kindly said,
"You see this street?
Go two blocks, and turn right.
And at the first traffic light, turn left.
There you will find a Korean church.
It would be much better for you and your family
to join that church!"
When I heard this,
I envisioned the pastor's face.
What kind of expression would you see on his face?
I see the fear of diversity!
. . .

The people in the story of the tower of Babel,
who were so afraid of losing their homogeneity
in race and language,
decided to build a city and a high tower in it to protect themselves.
Like them,
the pastor might be fearful of
breaking the ethnic and cultural unity of his congregation.
He probably thought he was accomplishing something
that seemed to be good—
a unified, stable congregation,
"lest [it] be scattered."
We know, however,
that in the story of the tower of Babel,
God was not so happy about
the people's desire to be a unified group.
So God confused their language
to stop the construction of the city and the tower,
and scattered the people over the face of the entire earth.
. . .

Is diversity a curse from God to be feared
or a blessing from God to be celebrated?
World history witnesses to
how horrible the human desire to be unified is.
Although in the biblical story,
God *did* scatter the homogeneous group
to become diversified communities,
people have continuously kept on trying
to build up their own cities and towers,
to exercise the power of control,
all in fear of diversity.
And their attempts have created numerous horrible consequences,
such as ethnic genocide, racial cleansing,
and divisions within religious communities.
The tragic history of 9/11 serves as an example of
how this horror continues to this day.

. . .

I remember Paul the apostle,
the apostle of Christian diversity.
He must have understood the story of the tower of Babel
as the story of God's grace,
in which diversity was granted as a genuine blessing
for human communities.
According to Paul's Letter to the Romans,
the dividing walls of the city and
the controlling power of the tower of Babel
have already been destroyed in Jesus Christ.
God has designed and created
a new community in Jesus Christ,
and diversity has been given to the people as grace-gifts,
in Greek, *charismata*.
Paul called this community *ekklēsia*, the church,
which belongs to the "body of Christ."
During Paul's time,
the metaphor "body" was used
in Greco-Roman political philosophy
as a way of stressing the importance of all the different factions of a city,
such as different ethnic groups and trade guilds.
The word "body" symbolized the cooperation of citizens
for the sake of a city's safety and prosperity,
by living together in harmony.
Paul took the metaphor of body
as the prime image for the church,

to have the same effect.
He says that we are baptized into one body,
the body of Christ,
in which the diversity of grace-gifts, *charismata*, is valued,
and unity and harmony are fulfilled.
The church as the body of Christ is called to live in harmony,
to discern "the will of God—
what is good and acceptable and perfect"—
in mutual agreement and with sober judgment.
By worshiping God in diversity
and testifying in the world
to the beauty of the diversity of God's people,
the church exists in the world to be a transforming agent.

. . .

While in Korea,
I learned that some Christian churches and organizations
are playing this role of a transforming agent
by practicing the ministry of diversity.
They were the first groups in Korea
to become aware of the suffering of migrant workers
and other victims of globalization.
In response,
they embraced the marginalized people in their ministries,
crossing the boundaries of race, culture, and language differences.
I've also learned
that some American churches have proclaimed
the good news of diversity in Jesus Christ
and have been working hard and skillfully as transforming agencies
by serving people varied in race, gender, class, and sexuality.

. . .

But we all know that the ministry of diversity in Jesus Christ
is *not* an easy one
because the gospel of diversity in Jesus Christ threatens
our traditional identities,
which are dependent on
race, nationality, and social and economic status.
It challenges us to reorient our identities to the fact
that we all bear the image of God.
In many ways,
the ministry of diversity requires us
to be courageous and patient.
It is a radical challenge for both the pastor and her congregation.

. . .

The Rev. Martha,
who was appointed to a Methodist church
in downtown Atlanta, Georgia,
had a radical vision for her church,
changing it from a patriarchal and racially homogeneous group
to an egalitarian, multiracial family.
But not all the members of her congregation
were happy about her vision.
One day,
a man in the church called her up to tell her
that if she took in another person of color,
he was leaving the church,
and he would take everything he had given the church with him.
If he left, that meant
he would take about thirty-five others with him,
mostly his relatives.
The following Sunday morning,
Rev. Martha took in another minority family anyway.
During her first year,
the membership dropped 20 percent.
One year later, however,
the membership gained the entire 20 percent back
and has been steadily increasing since then with newcomers
from different ethnic groups.
Those who stayed later shared their feelings, saying,
"Our people were afraid,
afraid of ourselves, being from different races,
afraid of ourselves, being from different cultures.
But in the midst of our fears,
God has surprised us and blessed us.
The diversity that we feared has empowered us
to accept God's truth in the world."

. . .

What a wonderful surprise to celebrate diversity like this!
It reminds me of my own experience in Korea.
One of the schools where I taught in Korea last fall was
my alma mater, Ewha Woman's University,
which, I think, is the largest women's institution in the world,
with thirty thousand female students.
Its divinity school has a global ministry program
that invites future female church leaders
from developing countries in Asia and Africa
to study for advanced degrees.

I had the honor of teaching a group of these international women,
who came from Myanmar, China, and Thailand.
Our theological conversations in class were global—
multilingual, multiperspective, and definitely multicontextual.
And surprisingly,
during each class,
we all felt the rich, stimulating, and provoking energy of the Spirit!
The Spirit of God freed us from
the coercive, controlling power of the tower of Babel
and empowered us to envision a "different world"
for the present and the future.

. . .

Is a different world possible in our age of globalization,
a world in which justice and peace are truly global?
Can a different world be possible
in which different people find themselves at home together
living harmoniously, respecting one another,
celebrating God's jubilee?
As long as we can continue to find
surprising stories of God's blessing through diversity,
I dare to say,
"Yes, a different world is possible!
Because the Spirit of God is at work among us,
creating a beautiful new world based on diversity!"
I am looking forward to your surprising stories
within and beyond the church!

Dear Mary and Elizabeth

Luke 1:39–56

This sermon was created for preaching at the Women of Color Preaching Festival held at the National Cathedral College of Preachers in Washington, DC. The listeners were female preachers and clergy from many different ethnic communities in the United States. In the sermon, there are three major movements: First, the appreciation of the text as the extraordinary childbearing story of two Jewish women, Mary and Elizabeth, in first-century Judea; second, the song Magnificat, sung by a laywoman as a response to the question raised from the story; and last, the letter to Mary and Elizabeth, in which the preacher appeals to them for the sake of her and her listeners' lives, in order to follow in their footsteps. The narrative and Mary's song in the text function as a paradigm of Christian discipleship for contemporary listeners. Mary and Elizabeth's childbearing is interpreted as an extraordinary event, which participates in God's humanizing activity. It creates a vivid contrast with the ordinary feminine activity of childbearing. The letter to Mary and Elizabeth appeals to the aesthetic dimension of the listeners with symbolic and poetic language. It represents their voices from deep within their hearts, as a faithful and honest response to God's invitation to God's extraordinary business.

TEXT

In those days Mary set out and went with haste to a Judean town in the hill country, where she entered the house of Zechariah and greeted Elizabeth. When Elizabeth heard Mary's greeting, the child leaped in her womb. And Elizabeth was filled with the Holy Spirit and exclaimed with a loud cry, "Blessed are you among women, and blessed is the fruit of your womb. And why has this happened to me, that the mother of my Lord comes to me? For as soon as I heard the sound of your greeting, the child in my womb leaped for joy. And blessed is she who believed that there would be a fulfillment of what was spoken to her by the Lord." And Mary said,

> "My soul magnifies the Lord,
>   and my spirit rejoices in God my Savior,
> for he has looked with favor on the lowliness of his servant.
>   Surely, from now on all generations will call me blessed;
> for the Mighty One has done great things for me,
>   and holy is his name.
> His mercy is for those who fear him
>   from generation to generation.
> He has shown strength with his arm;
>   he has scattered the proud in the thoughts of their hearts.
> He has brought down the powerful from their thrones,
>   and lifted up the lowly;
> he has filled the hungry with good things,
>   and sent the rich away empty.
> He has helped his servant Israel,
>   in remembrance of his mercy,
> according to the promise he made to our ancestors,
>   to Abraham and to his descendants forever."

And Mary remained with her about three months and then returned to her home. (Luke 1:39–56)

SERMON

The unique feature of the Gospel of Luke is that
it begins with the story of two pregnant women,
Mary, the mother of Jesus,
and Elizabeth, the mother of John the Baptist.

Mary and Elizabeth are relatives
and became pregnant within six months of each other.
Luke describes their pregnancies as fairly unusual events.
Mary is young, single, and virgin;
Elizabeth is too old to be pregnant,
near or past menopause.
However, by divine intervention,
both women become pregnant:
The angel Gabriel visited Mary
and told her God's plan for her
to become the mother of Jesus, the Son of God.
Six months earlier,
Elizabeth's husband was also visited by an angel
and learned that his wife would bear a child
who would guide the people of Israel to the Lord, their God.

. . .

From the perspective of first-century Jewish society,
Mary's out-of-wedlock pregnancy is obviously immoral.
How can she explain her mysterious pregnancy
to her fiancé and family members?
She will be publicly disgraced in front of her neighbors
as she begins to show.
Different from Mary,
for Elizabeth,
her pregnancy may bring her exuberant joy
because she is ashamed of her barrenness.
In her society,
the most significant responsibility for a woman
was to continue the family line
by bearing a son.
But for a long time,
Elizabeth was not able to fulfill this feminine duty.
In spite of Elizabeth's joy for her pregnancy,
can you imagine how hard it would be
to bear one's first child at such an old age?
I have two children.
My first is an eighteen-year-old daughter,
going to college this fall.
My second child is a three-year-old son.
I was pregnant with him at the age of forty-two.
This second pregnancy was much more difficult for me
because of my age.
My body was not strong enough to hold my little one
until he reached full term.

Thus he was born at only eight months.
I wonder if Elizabeth and Mary's sons went through
the "terrible twos" and later a rebellious puberty.
Perhaps not, considering that
they lived unique lives led by the Holy Spirit.
But their teaching and proclamation
of the kingdom of God in a manner
that was upside down from the world order of the times
drove them to be killed
at early ages
by the worldly authorities.
Have you ever experienced
how painful it is to lose children, at any age,
even if they died for valiant reasons?
A Korean proverb says that
when children die, their parents bury them in their hearts,
for they carry the pain for the rest of their lives.
Can you imagine Mary's and Elizabeth's sorrow and pain
when they lost their children?
Elizabeth may have been traumatized for a while
because of her innocent son's death notice.
Mary may have fainted at the foot of her son's cross
because of her heart-stricken pangs.
. . .
Despite these potential risks and difficulties,
An inherent part of the divine offer to have children,
Mary and Elizabeth joyfully accept the divine offer
with a determined "yes."
Why did they answer "yes" to such a dangerous offer?
In response to this question,
Mary sings a song:

(*The preacher yields the preaching place to the female singer and stands behind her or sits in the preacher's chair in the chancel while the Magnificat is sung.*)

1. My soul gives glory to my God,
    My heart pours out its praise.
   God lifted up my lowliness
    In many marvelous ways.
2. My God has done great things for me:
    Yes, holy is this name.

All people will declare me blessed,
and blessings they shall claim.
3. From age to age to all who fear,
Such mercy love imparts,
Dispensing justice far and near,
Dismissing selfish hearts.
4. Love casts the mighty from their thrones,
Promotes the insecure,
Leaves hungry spirits satisfied;
The rich seem suddenly poor.
5. Praise God, whose loving covenant
Supports those in distress,
Remembering past promises
With present faithfulness.
(paraphrased by Miriam Therese Winter)[3]

. . .

(After the song, the preacher returns to her preaching place and continues.)

Mary was a poor peasant woman,
living in predominantly Gentile Galilee,
a colony of the invincible Roman Empire,
struggling every day for survival and dignity.
Elizabeth was the lowest of the lowly,
suffering the tormenting bitterness of barrenness
by the severe reproach
of her household and neighbors.
How amazing it is that
God's dealing with the world is a reversal of the human order:
Against the proud, who are self-sufficient,
God chooses the humble and the lowly;
against the rich, who are accumulating wealth
at the expense of others,
God trusts the poor and those in need;
and against the powerful, who are satisfied
with the way things are,
God calls the powerless, who are anticipating
a renewal of the world.
Mary and Elizabeth were eagerly waiting for a future
that would be totally different
from the oppressive and unjust present.
For them,
their pregnancies with

the Son of God and the forerunner of the Messiah
were signs of the nearness of that future
they had been waiting for.
They were delighted and rejoiced in the divine offer
and joyfully said yes,
because they knew that the fulfillment of God's promise
for a new heaven and a new earth was very near,
a new world
in which "justice roll[s] down like a river" (Amos 5:24),
the proud are scattered,
the lowly are lifted up,
the hungry are fed,
and the rich are sent away empty-handed.
For Mary and Elizabeth,
God's offer for them to have children
was not simply a proposal to fulfill their stereotypical feminine roles
at a biological level,
but to become God's partners for an extraordinary business
to fulfill the promise of God on earth.
. . .

In honor of Mary and Elizabeth,
I have written a letter to them on behalf of all of us.
And I'd like to read it to you now:

(*The preacher shows an envelope to the congregation, addressed to "Ms.
Mary and Ms. Elizabeth," pulls out the letter from it, and reads.*)

Dear Mary and Elizabeth,
It's wonderful to hear your stories
recorded in the first chapter of the Gospel of Luke.
You may not realize how challenging it was,
what you did in your small, colonized territory of Judea,
about two thousand years ago.
We are living
on the opposite side of the planet,
in a vastly different environment from yours.
Our American society, a so-called democratic world,
has enhanced the status of women to be almost equal to men
in social and professional positions.
Women are no longer treated
as servants of men and of their households.
Childbearing is just one of many options for us.

If you visited our world,
you would be amazed to find many women
in top positions of every area of society—
on the congressional floor,
at the stock exchange,
in professional chairs,
on the benches of judgment,
and even behind the pulpit.
As unbelievable as it might seem,
our group is gathering
in a beautiful, sacred place
located in the capital of our nation
to learn how to enhance our voices
as female preachers.
We live in the most affluent society in human history.
We are neither poor nor lowly, as you were.
Rather, we, as American citizens,
are sitting quite comfortably at the top of
the world's economic pyramid.
But, ironically,
we must admit to you that
the larger world surrounding us is not so different from yours:
There are so many people
living in poverty-stricken conditions
as victims of ruthless neoliberal capitalism
and selfish individualism;
regional and international wars continue at a global level;
Violence is everywhere—
at home, at the workplace, and even in the ivory towers.
Honestly speaking,
our country is like the Roman Empire of your day.
We are often considered the proud and the powerful,
seated on the thrones of judgment of the world,
which really belongs to God.
No, we are not in a very good position
to sing your song with joy.
Many of us cannot dare to praise your God,
who favors the poor and the lowly.
But we know that
our world should not continue to be like this.
We are in desperate need of
hearing your song again and again.
Many of us cannot dare to call your God our God,

who is the Lord of Justice and peace.
But we know that
the God of the poor and the lowly is the same God
whom we believe in.

. . .

Sister Mary,
sing your song for us again and again
so that the Spirit of God may guide us and lead us to a new life.
Whoever we are,
and whatever we do in society,
we need the life-giving Spirit,
who has the power to open our eyes
to see suffering and pain in the world
and transform our ordinary business
into the extraordinary business of God's reign.
Sister Elizabeth,
Pray for us that we can envision the future of our world
in which justice rolls down like a river,
the proud are scattered,
the lowly are lifted up,
the hungry are fed,
and the rich are sent away empty-handed.
Mary and Elizabeth,
pray to the Spirit
to extend a divine offer to us,
an offer granted to you thousands of years ago,
so that we may live as true disciples of Christ
as fearlessly and compassionately as you did.

(Preached at "Solidarity in Christ," a
Women of Color Preaching Festival
at the Cathedral College of Preachers
in Washington, DC, May 3, 2007)

Notes

Introduction

1. Paul Lehmann, *Ethics in a Christian Context* (New York: Harper & Row, 1963), 85.
2. Gordon Kaufman, *An Essay on Theological Method* (Atlanta: Scholars Press, 1995), 12.
3. Ibid., 17.
4. Leonora Tubbs Tisdale, *Preaching as Local Theology and Folk Art* (Minneapolis: Fortress Press, 1997).
5. James R. Nieman and Thomas G. Rogers, *Preaching to Every Pew: Cross-Cultural Strategies* (Minneapolis: Fortress Press, 2001).

Chapter 1: Contextual Approaches to Preaching

1. For detailed criticism, see Leonora Tubbs Tisdale, *Preaching as Local Theology and Folk Art* (Minneapolis: Fortress Press, 1997), 19.
2. Cf. Augustine, *On Christian Doctrine*, trans. D. W. Robertson Jr. (New York: Macmillan Publishing Co., 1958), book 4.
3. Among recent books on homiletics, Lucy Lind Hogan and Robert Reid, *Connecting with the Congregation: Rhetoric and the Art of Preaching* (Nashville: Abingdon Press, 1999), represents the speaker-oriented rhetorical approach to preaching.
4. Fred B. Craddock, *As One without Authority* (Nashville: Abingdon Press, 1971).
5. The New Homiletics intends to create an experience and an event for the listeners. Cf. James R. Nieman and Thomas G. Rogers, *Preaching to Every Pew: Cross-Cultural Strategies* (Minneapolis: Fortress Press, 2001), 17.
6. Ibid., 57–64.
7. E.g., James Hopewell, *Congregation: Stories and Structures* (Philadelphia: Fortress Press, 1987); Nancy T. Ammerman et al., *Studying Congregations: A New Handbook* (Nashville: Abingdon Press, 1998); W. Paul Jones, *World within a Congregation: Dealing with Theological Diversity* (Nashville: Abingdon Press, 2000).
8. Robert J. Schreiter, *Constructing Local Theologies* (Maryknoll: Orbis Books, 1986).
9. Ibid., 38.

10. Ibid., 32.

11. Ibid., 60.

12. Ibid., 33.

13. Ibid., 124.

14. Ibid., 16.

15. Ibid., 51.

16. Ibid., 54.

17. Clifford Geertz, *The Interpretation of Culture* (New York: Basic Books, 1973), 89, quoted in Tisdale, *Preaching as Local Theology*, 12.

18. Tisdale, *Preaching as Local Theology*, 15.

19. Ibid., 15–16.

20. Ibid., 77.

21. Ibid., 64–77.

22. Kathryn Tanner, *Theories of Culture: Guides to Theological Inquiry* (Minneapolis: Fortress Press, 1997), 42.

23. Ibid., 38.

24. Ibid., 42.

25. Ibid., 43.

26. Tisdale, *Preaching as Local Theology*, 17, 63.

27. Ibid., 56.

28. Daniel Chandler, *Semiotics: The Basics* (London: Routledge, 2002), 2.

29. Ibid., 3.

30. Ibid., 14.

31. Ibid.

32. Tisdale, *Preaching as Local Theology*, 33.

33. The twelve questions are included in Nieman and Rogers, *Preaching to Every Pew*, 19.

34. Ibid., 8.

35. Ibid., 10.

36. Ibid., 13.

37. Ibid.

38. Ibid.

39. Ibid., 13–14.

40. Ibid., 14.

41. Ibid., 15.

42. Ibid.

43. Ibid., 16.

44. Ibid., 147.

45. Ibid.

46. Ibid., 148.

47. Ibid., 150.

48. Tanner, *Theories of Culture*, 58.

49. Nieman and Rogers, *Preaching to Every Pew*, 13.

50. Cf. Eph. 2; 1 Cor. 12; and Rom. 12.

51. Joseph R. Jeter Jr. and Ronald J. Allen, *One Gospel, Many Ears: Preaching for Different Listeners in the Congregation* (St. Louis: Chalice Press, 2002).

52. Nieman and Rogers, *Preaching to Every Pew*, 153.

53. Ibid.

54. Robert J. Schreiter, *The New Catholicity: Theology between the Global and the Local* (Maryknoll, NY: Orbis Books, 1997).

55. Ibid., 5.

56. Ibid., 8, 11.

57. Ibid., 12.

58. Marc Cortez, "Creation and Context: A Theological Framework for Contextual Theology," *Westminster Theological Journal* 67 (2005): 360.

Chapter 2: Globalization and the Context for Preaching

1. Daniel Hardy, "The Spirit of God in Creation and Reconciliation," in *Christ and Context*, ed. Hilary D. Regan and Alan J. Torrance (Edinburgh: T&T Clark, 1993), 242–46.

2. Rebecca Chopp and Mark Taylor, eds., *Reconstructing Christian Theology* (Minneapolis: Fortress Press, 1994), 7.

3. Marjorie Suchocki, *God, Christ, Church: A Practical Guide to Process Theology* (New York: Crossroad, 1989), 61.

4. Paul Lehmann, *Ethics in a Christian Context* (New York: Harper & Row, 1963), 59.

5. Paul Lehmann, *The Decalogue and a Human Future: The Meaning of the Commandments for Making and Keeping Human Life Human* (Grand Rapids: Wm. B. Eerdmans Publishing Co., 1995), 11.

6. Lehmann, *Ethics in a Christian Context*, 72.

7. Ibid., 72–73.

8. Ibid., 112.

9. Ibid., 117.

10. Daniel Migliore, *Faith Seeking Understanding: An Introduction to Christian Theology* (Grand Rapids: Wm. B. Eerdmans Publishing Co., 1991), 24.

11. Christian D. Pohl, "Hospitality from the Edge: The Significance of Marginality in the Practice of Welcome," *The Annual of the Society of Christian Ethics*, ed. Harlan Beckley (Boston: Society of Christian Ethics, 1995), 122.

12. Jung Young Lee, *Marginality: The Key to Multicultural Theology* (Minneapolis: Fortress Press, 1995), 60.

13. Ibid., 61.

14. Roland Robertson, "Globalization and the Future of 'Traditional Religion,'" in *God and Globalization*, vol. 1, *Religion and the Powers of the Common Life*, ed. Max L. Stackhouse and Peter J. Paris (Harrisburg, PA: Trinity Press International, 2000), 66.

15. Ronald Robertson and Jan Aart Scholte, eds., *The Encyclopedia of Globalization*, vol. 2 (New York: Routledge, 2007), 521.

16. Ibid., 524–25.

17. Ibid., 526.

18. Abdullahi A. An-Na'im, "The Politics of Religion and the Morality of Globalization," in *Religion in Global Civil Society*, ed. Mark Juergensmeyer (Oxford: Oxford University Press, 2005), 33.

19. Robertson and Scholte, *Encyclopedia of Globalization*, 2:526.

20. Rosemary R. Ruether, *Integrating Ecofeminism, Globalization, and World Religions* (Lanham, MD: Rowman & Littlefield Publishers, 2005), 33.

21. Ibid.

22. Ibid., 34–35.

23. Ibid., 92.

24. The World Bank and its sister organization, the International Monetary Fund, were created at Bretton Woods, New Hampshire, in 1944. Together they are referred to as the Bretton Woods Institutions, or BWIs.

25. Ruether, *Integrating Ecofeminism*, 160–63.

26. Ibid., 4–6.

27. Ibid., 9.

28. Ibid., 94; M. Douglas Meeks, "Global Economy and the Globalization of Theological Education," in *The Globalization of Theological Education,* ed. Alice F. Evans, Robert F. Evans, and David A. Roozen (Maryknoll, NY: Orbis Books, 1993), 252.

29. Ruether, *Integrating Ecofeminism*, 7.

30. See http://devdata.worldbank.org/wdi2005/Section1_1_1.htm.

31. Ruether, *Integrating Ecofeminism*, 146.

32. Meeks, "Global Economy," 248; Jürgen Moltmann, *God for a Secular Society: The Public Relevance of Theology* (Minneapolis: Fortress Press, 1999), 67.

33. Moltmann, *God for a Secular Society,* 66.

34. Ruether, *Integrating Ecofeminism,* 7.

35. Jon P. Guinnemann, "Property and Sacred Ordering in Global Civil Society," in Juergensmeyer, *Religion in Global Civil Society*, 107–9. Transnational corporations that commodify natural resources are, for example, Vivendi Universal, a French company providing water supply and distribution; DuPont, a U.S.-based chemical company owning a large number of patents on genetic resource; and Monsanto, a huge multinational company in seeds, food, and agribusiness owning patents on genetic seeds.

36. Robert Schreiter explains the "root metaphor" as a symbolic language that "gives direction to the signs to be included and the codes to be developed . . . It provides the major linkage between the sign systems of a culture, . . . to create a cultural whole." Robert Schreiter, *Constructing Local Theology* (Maryknoll, NY: Orbis Books, 1986), 69–70.

37. Ibid., 69, 73.

38. Thomas Long, *Beyond the Worship Wars: Building Vital and Faithful Worship* (Bethesda, MD: Alban Institute, 2001), 7–8.

39. Robertson and Scholte, *Encyclopedia of Globalization*, 1:259.

40. Ibid., 2:527.

41. See *New York Times*, January 21, 2007, http://www.nytimes.com/2007/01/21/us/21fugees.html.

42. Ibid.

43. Elizabeth M. Bounds and Bobbi Patterson, "Intercultural Understanding in a Community School," in Juergensmeyer, *Religion in Global Civil Society*, 175.

44. Ibid., 179–80.

45. Ibid., 176.

46. Ibid., 180.

47. Robertson and Scholte, *Encyclopedia of Globalization*, 2:64.

48. Charles R. Foster and Theodore Brelsford, *We Are the Church Together: Cultural Diversity in Congregational Life* (Valley Forge, PA: Trinity Press International, 1996), 17.

49. Gerardo Marti, *A Mosaic of Believers: Diversity and Innovation in a Multiethnic Church* (Bloomington: Indiana University Press, 2005), 2.

50. Ibid., 23.

51. Ibid., 2.

52. A Report of Working Group 1 of the Intergovernmental Panel on Climate Change, Summary for Policymakers, 10. Available on http://www.ipcc-wg1.unibe.ch/publications/wg1-ar4/wg1-ar4.html (10/26/2009).

53. Ibid., 13.

54. http://en.wikipedia.org/wiki/List_of_countries_by_carbon_dioxide_emissions (10/26/2009).

55. Ruether, *Integrating Ecofeminism*, 13.

56. Moltmann, *God for a Secular Society*, 93.

57. "Global Melting, Big Thaw," *National Geographic Magazine*, June 2007, http://ngm.nationalgeographic.com/2007/26/big-thaw-text (10/26/2009); emphasis is added.

58. *New York Times*, May 24, 2007, Global Warming in the section of Science; cf. A Report of Working Group 1 of the Intergovernmental Panel on Climate Change, 14.

59. Robert K. Schaeffer, *Understanding Globalization: The Social Consequences of Political, Economic, and Environmental Change* (Lanham, MD: Rowman & Littlefield Publishers, 2005), 299, 303. Annually 50,000 to 60,000 people, primarily young children, in the United States die of respiratory problems caused by carbon dioxide.

60. National Public Radio, www.indiaresource.org/news/2008/1051.html (10/26/2009).

61. Virginia R. Burkett, David B. Zilkoski, and David A. Hart, "Sea-Level Rise and Subsidence Implications for Flooding in New Orleans, Louisiana," Abstract, 63. www.nwrc.usgs.gov/hurricane/Sea-Level-Rise.pdf (10/26/2009).

62. Dinyar Godrej, *The No-Nonsense Guide to Climate Change* (Oxford: New Internationalist Publications, 2001), 112; quoted in Ruether, *God for a Secular Society*, 15.

63. Schaeffer, *Understanding Globalization*, 300.

64. Ibid.

65. Ibid., 301.

66. Ibid., 299–302.

67. Jürgen Osterhammel and Niels P. Peterson, *Globalization: A Short History*, trans. Dona Geyer (Princeton, NJ: Princeton University Press, 2005), 9.

68. Ronald Cole-Turner, "Science, Technology, and the Mission of Theology in a New Century," in *God and Globalization*, vol. 2, *The Spirit and the Modern Authorities*, ed. Max L. Stackhouse and Don S. Browning (Harrisburg, PA: Trinity Press International, 2001), 144.

69. Ibid., 147.

70. Nathan D. Mitchell, "Ritual and New Media," in *Cyberspace-Cyberethics-Cybertheology*, ed. Eric Borgman, Stephan van Erp, and Hille Haker (London: SCM Press, 2005), 92.

71. Yersu Kim, "Philosophy and the Prospects for a Universal Ethics," in Stackhouse and Paris, *God and Globalization*, 1:86.

72. Eric Borgman and Stephan Van Erp, "Which Message Is the Medium? Concluding Remarks on Internet, Religion and the Ethics of Mediated Connectivity," in Borgman, Erp, and Haker, *Cyberspace-Cyberethics-Cybertheology*, 109.

73. Cole-Turner, "Science, Technology," 144.

74. Ibid., 145. The term "virtual communities" means social aggregations that emerge from webs of personal relationships in cyberspace.

75. Robertson and Scholte, *Encyclopedia of Globalization*, 4:1235. "Virtual reality" means the enhanced interpersonal simulations of reality through technology such as multiuser domains and chat rooms.

76. In the 2002 presidential election in South Korea, the Internet actually generated profound changes with regard to the results of the political campaigns. The former president, Roh Moo Hyun, used the online newspaper Web site, OhmyNews, which is regarded as the first of its kind in the world (http://en.wikipedia.org/wiki/OhmyNews), to communicate with constituents, and his online campaign had swung the presidential election by stirring tens of thousands of the young generation to support him and his party. In that year, almost 70 percent of homes in Korea had Internet service, compared with about 5 percent in Britain (www.guardian.co.uk/technology/2003/feb/24/newmedia.koreanews) (October 24, 2009). The election of Barack Obama as president has echoed that of Roh Moo Hyun. Mr. Obama's campaign used the Internet not only for fundraising but also for

organizing supporters, advertising to voters, and defending against attacks (www
.newamerica.net/publications/articles/2009/world_wide_webbed_12896) (October 24, 2009).

77. Mitchell, "Ritual and New Media," 91.

78. "Reflexivity" refers to "the ways in which social actors reflect upon and
learn from the circumstances in which they find themselves at any point in time."
See Robertson and Scholte, *Encyclopedia of Globalization*, 3:1229.

Chapter 3: Humanization and Transcontextual Preaching

1. Paul Lehmann, *Ethics in a Christian Context* (New York: Harper & Row,
1963), 117, 47.

2. Elsa Tamez, "Neoliberalism and Christian Freedom: A Reflection on the
Letter to the Galatians," in *Revolution of Spirit: Ecumenical Theology in Global
Context*, ed. Nantawan Boonprasat Lewis (Grand Rapids: Wm. B. Eerdmans
Publishing Co., 1998), 112.

3. Gordon D. Kaufman, *God, Mystery, Diversity: Christian Theology in a Pluralistic World* (Minneapolis: Fortress Press, 1996), 121.

4. Ibid., 121–22.

5. Sallie McFague, *Models of God: Theology for an Ecological, Nuclear Age*
(Philadelphia: Fortress Press, 1987), 53.

6. Ibid., 72, 73, 77.

7. Ibid., 72–73.

8. Daniel L. Migliore, "The Trinity and the Theology of Religions," in *God's
Life in Trinity*, ed. Miroslav Volf and Michael Welker (Minneapolis: Fortress
Press, 2006), 106.

9. M. Douglas Meeks, "The Social Trinity and Property," in Volk and
Welker, *God's Life in Trinity*, 14.

10. Miroslav Volf, "Exclusion and Embrace: Theological Reflections in the
Wake of 'Ethnic Cleansing,'" *Journal of Ecumenical Studies* 29, no. 2 (Spring
1992): 248.

11. Meeks, "Social Trinity," 226 n. 10, citing Leonardo Boff, *Trinity and
Society* (Maryknoll, NY: Orbis Books, 1986), 6, 8.

12. Volf, "Exclusion and Embrace," 248.

13. Gordon D. Kaufman, *Jesus and Creativity* (Minneapolis: Fortress Press,
2006), 64–65, 68.

14. David H. Kelsey, "Wisdom, Theological Anthropology, and Modern Secular Interpretation of Humanity," in Volk and Welker, *God's Life in Trinity*, 44–60.

15. Ibid., 54.

16. Ibid., 57.

17. Volf, "Exclusion and Embrace," 235.

18. Ibid., 237.

19. Jon Sobrino, "Redeeming Globalization through Its Victims," in *Globalization and Its Victims*, ed. Jon Sobrino and Felix Wilfred (London: SCM Press, 2001), 111.

20. Volf, "Exclusion and Embrace," 247–48.

21. Thomas E. Reynolds, *The Broken Whole: Philosophical Steps toward a Theology of Global Solidarity* (Albany: State University of New York Press, 2006), 192.

22. Ibid., 194.

23. Volf, "Exclusion and Embrace," 241.

24. Harvey G. Cox Jr., "Make Way for the Spirit," in Volk and Welker, *God's Life in Trinity*, 98.

25. Lehmann, *Ethics in a Christian Context*, 83.

26. Ibid.

27. Ibid., 85.

28. Paul Lehmann, *The Transfiguration of Politics* (New York: Harper & Row, 1975), 7.

29. Ibid.

30. Lehmann, *Ethics in a Christian Context*, 85, quoting Eph. 3:8–11; 4:13 RSV.

31. McFague, *Models of God*, 46.

32. Ibid.

33. Migliore, "The Trinity and the Theology," 114.

34. Ibid., 112.

35. See Leonora Tubbs Tisdale, *Preaching as Local Theology and Folk Art* (Minneapolis: Fortress Press, 1997).

36. Reynolds, *The Broken Whole*, 171.

37. Ibid., 85.

38. Ibid., 87.

39. Ibid.

40. Michel Foucault, "Polemics, Politics, and Problemizations," in *The Foucault Reader*, ed. Paul Rabinow (New York: Pantheon Books, 1984), 381–82; quoted in Reynolds, *The Broken Whole*, 70.

41. Reynolds, *The Broken Whole*, 94.

42. Ibid., 89.

43. Ibid., 195.

44. William Morris, ed., *The American Heritage Dictionary of the English Language* (Boston: American Heritage Publishing Co., 1975), 63.

45. Paul Lehmann, *The Decalogue and a Human Future: The Meaning of the Commandments for Making and Keeping Human Life Human* (Grand Rapids: Wm. B. Eerdmans Publishing Co., 1995), 23.

46. Ibid.

47. Ibid.

48. Ibid., 24.

49. José Ignacio González Faus, "The Utopia of the Human Family: The Universalization of the Truly Human as Real Globalization," in Sobrino and Wilfred, *Globalization and Its Victims*, 100.

50. Ibid.

51. Ibid., 101.

52. Ibid.

53. Ibid., 101–2.

54. Meeks, "Social Trinity," 18–20.

55. Ibid., 19.

56. Ibid., 16, 21.

57. On November 30, 1999, more than 50,000 people gathered in Seattle to protest the Millennial summit of the World Trade Organization; and during September 10–14, 2003, some 10,000 protesters demonstrated in Cancún, Mexico. In addition, numerous antiglobalization movements have sprung up in other cities in the world, including the World Social Forum in Porto Alegre, Brazil, in 2001, 2002, and 2003, and in Mumbai, India, in 2004, and other direct action campaigns and networks against globalization such as the Our Sister Parish network in El Salvador and the Via Campesina network and the Sem Terra [Landless] movement in Brazil. For more information, see Rosemary Radford Ruether, *Integrating Ecofeminism, Globalization, and World Religions* (Lanham, MD: Rowman & Littlefield Publishers, 2005), 131–59.

58. Richard Lischer, *The End of Words* (Grand Rapids: Wm. B. Eerdmans Publishing Co., 2005), 163.

59. Lehmann, *Ethics in a Christian Context*, 85.

60. This sermon is attached to this volume, as shown on the contents pages above.

61. William Hull, *Strategic Preaching: The Role of the Pulpit in Pastoral Leadership* (St. Louis: Chalice Press, 2006), 118.

62. Ibid., 119.

63. Ibid., 2.

64. Ibid., 12.

65. Ibid., 192.

66. Ibid., 164.

67. Ibid.

68. Ibid., 120.

69. The Doctor of Ministry Program of the Iliff School of Theology, where I am serving as director, focuses on Preaching in the Practice of Ministry and requires first-year students to organize their sermon-formation-and-feedback group with diverse members of their congregations, if possible, from different race, gender, age, ethnicity, sexuality, theological orientation, and so forth. The students have responded very positively to the functioning of this group in their preaching ministry.

70. Hull, *Strategic Preaching*, 120.

71. Lischer, *The End of Words*, 44.

Chapter 4: Transcontextual Hermeneutics

1. Paul Lehmann, *Ethics in a Christian Context* (New York: Harper & Row, 1963), 316.

2. Ibid.

3. David Lochhead, *The Liberation of the Bible* (Thornbury, ON: Student Christian Movement of Canada, 1977), 28.

4. Ibid.

5. Cf. Fernando F. Segovia and Mary Ann Tolbert, eds., *Reading from This Place*, 2 vols. (Minneapolis: Fortress Press, 1993–95); Elizabeth Schüssler Fiorenza, *Bread Not Stone: The Challenge of Feminist Biblical Interpretation* (Boston: Beacon Press, 1984); Cain Hope Felder, ed., *Stony the Road We Trod: African American Biblical Interpretation* (Minneapolis: Fortress Press, 1991); Fernando F. Segovia, ed., *Interpreting beyond Borders* (Sheffield: Sheffield Academic Press Ltd, 2000).

6. Mary Hess, "The Bible and Popular Culture," in *New Paradigms for Bible Study: The Bible in the Third Millennium*, ed., Robert M. Fowler, Edith Blumhofer, and Fernando F. Segovia (New York: T&T Clark International, 2004), 208.

7. Emmanuel Lévinas, *Totality and Infinity: An Essay on Exteriority* (Pittsburgh: Duquesne University Press, 1969), 47; quoted in Jeffrey Murray, "An Other-Burkean Frame: Rhetorical Criticism and the Call of the Other," *Communication Studies* 54, no. 2 (Summer 2003): 170.

8. Victor Turner, *The Forest of Symbols: Aspects of Ndembu Ritual* (Ithaca, NY: Cornell University Press, 1967, reprinted 1973), 95.

9. Ibid., 97.

10. Ibid., 95.

11. Sang Hyun Lee, "Claiming Our Liminal Spaces," *The Princeton Seminary Bulletin* 27, no. 3 (2006): 193.

12. Ibid., 195.

13. Ibid., 193.

14. Ibid., 194.

15. Hans-Georg Gadamer, *Truth and Method*, trans. Joel Weinsheimer and Donald G. Marshall, 2nd rev. ed. (New York: Crossroad, 1990), 374.

16. Charles R. Foster, *Embracing Diversity* (Bethesda, MD: Alban Institute, 1997), 95.

17. David Augsburger, *Pastoral Counseling across Cultures* (Philadelphia: Westminster Press, 1986), 28.

18. Ibid., 29.

19. Ibid., 30.

20. Richard Ward, *Speaking the Holy* (St. Louis: Chalice Press, 2002), 45.

21. David Rhoads, "Performing the Gospel of Mark," in *Body and the Bible: Interpreting and Experiencing Biblical Narrative*, ed. Björn Krondorfer (Philadelphia: Trinity Press International, 1992), 104.

22. Ibid., 105.

23. Cf., David Rhoads, "Performance Criticism: An Emerging Methodology in Second Testament Studies—Part II," *Biblical Theology Bulletin* 36, no. 4 (2006): 164–84.

24. Vernon Robbins, "Socio-Rhetorical Criticism: Mary, Elizabeth and the Magnificat as a Test Case," in *The New Literary Criticism and the New Testament*, ed. Edgar V. McKnight and Elizabeth Struthers Malbon (Valley Forge, PA: Trinity Press International, 1994), 194.

25. I borrow the term "a communitarian space" from Pablo Richard. He describes it as a new hermeneutical space in his essay "The Hermeneutics of Liberation: Theoretical Grounding for the Communitarian Reading of the Bible," in *Teaching the Bible: The Discourses and Politics of Biblical Pedagogy*, ed. Fernando F. Segovia and Mary Ann Tolbert (Maryknoll, NY: Orbis Books, 1998), 273.

26. Ibid.

27. James A. Sanders, *From Sacred Story to Sacred Text* (Philadelphia: Fortress Press, 1987), 66.

28. John McClure, *The Roundtable Pulpit: Where Leadership and Preaching Meet* (Nashville: Abingdon Press, 1995), 50.

29. George Aichele et al., *The Postmodern Bible* (New Haven: Yale University Press, 1995), 25.

30. Paul Ricoeur, *The Symbolism of Evil* (Boston: Beacon, 1969), 351.

31. Gamader, *Truth and Method*, 265–76; Lochhead, *Liberation of the Bible*, 25.

32. Paul Lehmann, *The Transfiguration of Politics* (New York: Harper & Row, 1975), 132.

33. Ricoeur, *Symbolism of Evil*, 351.

34. Thomas Kuhn, *The Structure of Scientific Revolutions* (Chicago: University of Chicago Press, 1970), 111.

35. Paul Ricoeur, "Biblical Hermeneutics," in *Paul Ricoeur on Biblical Hermeneutics*, ed. John Dominic Crossan, Semeia 4 (Missoula: Scholars Press, 1975), 75.

36. See Paul Lehmann, "Deliverance and Fulfillment: The Biblical View of Salvation," *Interpretation* 5, no. 4 (October 1951): 398; idem, *Transfiguration of Politics*; Garrett Green, *Imagining God: Theology and the Religious Imagination* (San Francisco: Harper & Row, 1989); Sanders, *From Sacred Story to Sacred Text*.

37. Sanders, *From Sacred Story to Sacred Text*, 73.

38. Lehmann, *Ethics in a Christian Context*, 122–23.

39. Ibid.

40. Gadamer, *Truth and Method*, 367.

41. For the full-length version of my interpretation, see *Feasting on the Word*, vol. 1 (Louisville, KY: Westminster John Knox Press, 2008), year B, Eighth Sunday after Epiphany.

42. For the full-length version of my interpretation, see *Feasting on the Word*, vol. 1 (Louisville, KY: Westminster John Knox Press, 2008), year B, Ninth Sunday after Epiphany.

43. Rhoads, "Performing the Gospel of Mark," 106.

44. Sharon D. Welch, *Communities of Resistance and Solidarity: A Feminist Theology of Liberation* (Maryknoll, NY: Orbis Books, 1985), 46.

45. Ibid., 91.

46. Lochhead, *Liberation of the Bible*, 48–49.

47. Cf. Deut. 22:23–24.

48. Cf. Deut. 22:13–29.

49. Klaus Wengst, *Pax Romana and the Peace of Jesus Christ* (Philadelphia: Fortress Press, 1987), 8–51.

50. See my book *Women Preaching: Theology and Practice through the Ages* (Cleveland: Pilgrim Press, 2004), chap. 5.

51. Robbins, "Socio-Rhetorical Criticism," 190.

52. Lehmann, *Ethics in a Christian Context*, 85.

Chapter 5: Negotiating Diversity

1. Cf. John S. McClure et al., *Listening to Listeners: Homiletical Case Studies* (St. Louis: Chalice Press, 2004); Joseph R. Jeter Jr. and Ronald J. Allen, *One Gospel, Many Ears: Preaching for Different Listeners in the Congregation* (St. Louis: Chalice Press, 2002); Andrew-Carl Wisdom, *Preaching to a Multi-generational Assembly* (Collegeville, MN: Liturgical Press, 2004); Lee McGee, *Wrestling with the Patriarchs: Retrieving Women's Voices in Preaching* (Nashville: Abingdon Press, 1996).

2. George Kennedy, *New Testament Interpretation through Rhetorical Criticism* (Chapel Hill: University of North Carolina Press, 1984), 5. I distinguish "rhetoric" from "rhetorical criticism." While the former focuses on creating a speech act, the latter aims to analyze and interpret written texts based on rhetorical elements.

3. Ibid., 34–35.

4. Ibid., 35.

5. Ibid., 9.

6. Ibid., 13–14.

7. Rebecca S. Chopp, "A Rhetorical Paradigm for Pedagogy," in *Teaching the Bible: The Discourses and Politics of Biblical Pedagogy*, ed. Fernando F. Segovia and Mary Ann Tolbert (Maryknoll, NY: Orbis Books, 1998), 303.

8. Ibid.

9. Elisabeth Schüssler Fiorenza, "The Ethics of Biblical Interpretation: Decentering Biblical Scholarship," *Journal of Biblical Literature* 107, no. 1 (1988): 15.

10. Aristotle, *The "Art" of Rhetoric*, trans. John Henry Freese, Loeb Classical Library 193 (London: William Heinemann, 1926).

11. M. Jimmie Killingsworth, *Appeals in Modern Rhetoric: An Ordinary-Language Approach* (Carbondale: Southern Illinois University Press, 2005), 15.

12. Anne Bishop, *Beyond Token Change: Breaking the Cycle of Oppression in Institutions* (Halifax, NS: Fernwood Publishing, 2005), 88–89.

13. Ibid., viii.

14. *Online Etymology Dictionary*, http://www.etymonline.com.

15. Killingsworth, *Appeals in Modern Rhetoric*, 2.

16. Ibid.

17. M. Jimmie Killingsworth and Jacqueline S. Palmer, *Ecospeak: Rhetoric and Environmental Politics in America* (Carbondale: Southern Illinois University Press, 1992), 17; quoted in Killingsworth, *Appeals in Modern Rhetoric*, vii.

18. Killingsworth, *Appeals in Modern Rhetoric*, 2.

19. Ibid., 13.

20. Augustine, *On Christian Doctrine*, trans. D. W. Robertson Jr. (New York: Macmillan Publishing Co., 1989), xviii.

21. Ibid., 136 (4.27).

22. Ibid., 137–38 (4.28, 29).

23. Ibid., 137 (4.28), 138 (4.29).

24. Ibid., 158 (4.51).

25. Lucy Atkinson Rose, *Sharing the Word: Preaching in the Roundtable Church* (Louisville, KY: Westminster John Knox Press, 1997), 95.

26. Ibid.

27. Ibid., 97.

28. Ibid., 96.

29. Ibid., 97.

30. Ibid., 100–101.

31. See dictionary.com, Unabridged (based on the Random House Unabridged Dictionary, 2006) under "aesthetics . . . used with a singular verb," nos. 1–2.

32. Edward Farley, *Faith and Beauty: A Theological Aesthetic* (Aldershot, UK: Ashgate, 2001), 117. Farley defines a "theological aesthetic" as a way to seek "to understand the place of beauty in the life of faith."

33. Ibid., 8.

34. Ibid., 6–8.

35. Ibid., 9.

36. Ibid., 11–12.

37. Longinus, *On the Sublime*, in *Critical Theory since Plato*, ed. Hazard Adams, rev. ed. (Fort Worth: Harcourt Brace Jovanovich College Publishers, 1992), 76 (I).

38. Ibid., 75.

39. Ibid.

40. James Martin Jr., *Beauty and Holiness: The Dialogue Between Aesthetics and Religion* (Princeton, NJ: Princeton University Press, 1990), 44.

41. Farley, *Faith and Beauty*, 37.

42. Ibid., 43.

43. Ibid., 45.

44. Karl Barth, *Church Dogmatics*, vol. 2, *The Doctrine of God*, part 1, ed. G. W. Bromiley and T. F. Torrance, trans. T. H. L. Parker et al. (Edinburgh: T&T Clark, 1957), 650.

45. William Dean, *Coming To: A Theology of Beauty* (Philadelphia: Westminster Press, 1972).

46. Ibid., 46.

47. Ibid., 48.

48. Ibid., 47.

49. Ibid., 60.

50. Ibid., 92.

51. Ibid., 106.

52. Ibid., 109.

53. Ibid., 111.

54. Cf. Rom. 10:15.

55. Dean, *Coming To*, 140.

56. Longinus, *On the Sublime*, 79 (VII).

57. Dean, *Coming To*, 115.

58. David Buttrick, *Homiletic: Moves and Structures* (Philadelphia: Fortress Press, 1987), 294.

59. Ibid., 55.

60. Ibid., 56.

61. Killingsworth, *Appeals in Modern Rhetoric*, 5.

62. Ibid., 28.

63. Ibid.

64. Ibid., 26.

65. Cf. Eugene Lowry, *The Homiletical Plot: The Sermon as Narrative Art Form* (Atlanta: John Knox Press, 1978).

66. Pierre Babin, *The New Era in Religious Communication* (Minneapolis: Fortress Press, 1991), 151.

67. Ibid., 149.

68. Thomas H. Troeger, *Imagining a Sermon* (Nashville: Abingdon Press, 1990), 72.

69. Killingsworth, *Appeals in Modern Rhetoric*, 35.

70. Young Pai, *Cultural Foundations of Education* (Columbus, OH: Merrill Publishing Co., 1990), 57.

71. Ibid., 58.

72. Grace S. Kim, "Asian North American Youth: A Ministry of Self-Identity and Pastoral Care," in *People on the Way: Asian North Americans Discovering Christ, Culture, and Community*, ed. David Ng (Valley Forge, PA: Judson Press, 1996), 205.

73. Ibid., 206.

74. Gerardo Marti, *A Mosaic of Believers: Diversity and Innovation in a Multiethnic Church* (Bloomington: Indiana University Press, 2005), 23.

75. Jung Young Lee, *Marginality: The Key to Multicultural Theology* (Minneapolis: Fortress Press, 1995), 98.

76. Eunjoo M. Kim, *Women Preaching: Theology and Practice through the Ages* (Cleveland: Pilgrim Press, 2004), 20.

77. Online Etymology Dictionary.

78. Kim, *Women Preaching*, 20.

79. Marjorie Suchocki, *God, Christ, Church: A Practical Guide to Process Theology* (New York: Crossroad, 1989), 3–4.

80. Jeffrey Murray, "An Other-Burkean Frame: Rhetorical Criticism and the Call of the Other," *Communication Studies* 54, no. 2 (Summer 2003): 184.

81. Martin Luther King Jr., "I Have a Dream," in *Contemporary American Public Discourse*, ed. H. R. Ryan, 3rd ed. (Prospect Heights, IL: Waveland Press, 1992), 216–17; quoted in Murray, "An Other-Burkean Frame," 184.

82. Troeger, *Imagining a Sermon*, 14–15.

Sermons

1. Thanks to my colleague, Richard Ward, for drafting this ensemble reading.

2. Thanks to my colleague, Catherine Kelsey, for drafting this ensemble reading.

3. This text of the Magnificat is from *The Presbyterian Hymnal* (Louisville, KY: Westminster/John Knox Press, 1990), 600; © Medical Mission Sisters 1978, 1987; used by permission.

Index

CPSIA information can be obtained
at www.ICGtesting.com
Printed in the USA
LVOW07s1135060817
544020LV00002B/277/P